Bill Perry

is the
Director of Training Materials
for InterFACE Ministries (Atlanta, GA).
He has 2 degrees in education
and has helped international students
since 1987.
The author of 5 other books,
he directs the
Florida Christmas Conference
and is an engaging speaker and trainer.
He lives with his wife
and 7 children in
Ft. Lauderdale, FL.

A Look Inside America

Bill Perry

A LOOK INSIDE AMERICA

by Bill Perry
InterFACE Ministries
3130 SW 21 Street
Ft. Lauderdale, FL 33312-3736
954-791-8854
Email: bill@billperry.tv

Published by Multi-Language Media, Inc.
PO Box 301, Ephrata PA 17522
717-738-0582
Email: mlminfo@multilanguage.com
www.multilanguage.com

Cover: Nate Krause
Statute of Liberty courtesy of Corbis Images
Satellite image courtesy of US Geological Survey

Clipart: Media Graphics International

NOTE: The author wishes to express his deep appreciation to Dr. Robert Kohls for his input, assistance and advice on this project.

4th Printing, 2008

ISBN 978-0-9633645-5-5

Contents

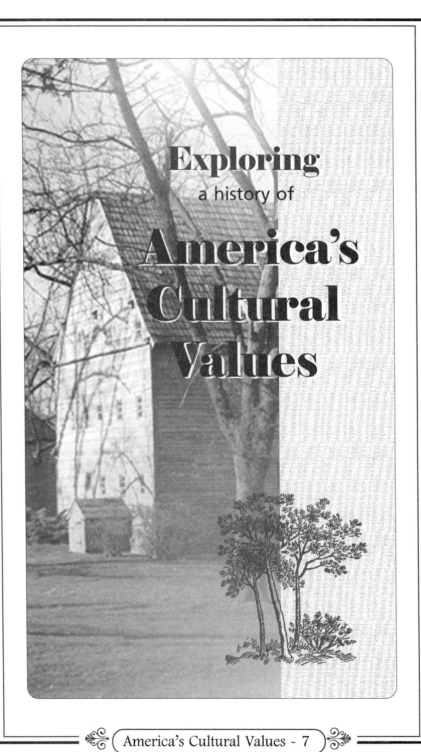

Exploring
a history of

America's
Cultural
Values

Exploring

a history of

America's Cultural Values

*Underlined words have definitions at the end of each article that are provided by *The Basic Newbury House Dictionary*. Definitions with an asterisk (*) are supplied by the author.

America's Cultural Values

Many visitors from overseas come to the United States every year. Most of them find American behaviors very different from what they see back home. Many international visitors think Americans are strange, unfriendly, self-centered and too busy. People in North America also appear to be more concerned about their time and the things they own rather than being concerned about people. How did Americans get this way? What ideas and values are important to Americans? To discover the answer, we must go back in time and consider how and when the United States began.

How did Americans get this way?

What ideas and values are important to Americans?

The 18th Century was an important period of time in the Western world. Europeans were learning new information from explorers about different peoples and cultures in other parts of the world. Scientists were making exciting discoveries. Creative thinkers were developing new inventions. Industry was just beginning. These events created a demand for changes in things like personal freedom, economics, government and business. The 1700's was an exciting time to be alive!

European settlers lived in North America for over 150 years before the colonists declared their independence from England in 1776. Some of the settlers came to find riches and success. But most of them came because they wanted to be free. Many wanted freedom to worship God. Some wanted to improve their lives. Others came to build new communities for the good of each other. Clearly they had certain ideas and beliefs in their minds. These ideas, and the opportunities they found in North America, formed the beginning of the unique cultural values that can be found in the US today.

The United States is a big country with the 4th largest population in the world and the 4th largest area of land. Immigrants from every country live in the US. Students from every country study in America. Yet there are certain cultural values that are widely accepted by the whole country. These values are those of the typical middle-class American. Other values can be found in smaller parts of the population. They come from groups of immigrants and ethnic minorities. However, middle-class American values still represent the main value system that people in the States follow. They are listed on the following page, along with contrasting values from other parts of the world.

American Values

1. Individualism

2. Equality / Fairness

3. Directness / Openness / Bluntness

4. Future Orientation

5. Control over the Environment

6. Change as Natural & Positive

7. Control over Time

8. Informality

9. Self-help / Personal Improvement

10. Competition

11. "Doing" Orientation & Achievements

12. Practicality / Efficiency / "Bottom Line"

13. Materialism

Other Values

1. Group Orientation

2. Rank / Status & Hierarchy

3. Indirectness / Saving "Face"

4. Past Orientation

5. Acceptance of Fate

6. Stability, Continuity & Tradition

7. Human Relationships / Harmony

8. Formality / <u>Protocol</u> / Ritual

9. Birthright Inheritance

10. Cooperation

11. "Being" Orientation

12. Philosophical Considerations

13. Spiritual Considerations

These American cultural values come from four main sources. They are:

> [1] The Protestant Reformation
>   (16th and 17th Centuries)
> [2] The Enlightenment
>   (18th Century)
> [3] The Industrial Revolution
>   (18th and 19th Centuries)
> [4] The Westward Movement (called "Manifest Destiny")
>   (17th through 19th Centuries)

Within these four sources are religion, philosophy, politics, culture and science. They all mixed together at an important time in North America as <u>immigrants</u> and <u>pioneers</u> settled a new land and built a new country. Let's look at each of these sources in historical order and see how they affected the thinking and culture of the United States. In the following sections you will find the American values in **bold** letters.

The Protestant Reformation
(16th & 17th Centuries)

The <u>Protestant Reformation</u> was a movement that began in 1517 AD. In that year Roman Catholic priest Martin Luther (1483-1546) disagreed with (or *protested* against) some teachings of the Catholic Church. Luther believed that people should have freedom to choose their own religious faith. Thus religious beliefs should only be accepted by personal choice, not by force. He thought too many religious ideas were forced on people, so he wanted to re-form the church's teachings. But four years later the Catholic Church removed Luther from the church. Friends in Germany <u>supported</u> him while he studied and wrote about many topics.

One of those topics was the idea of separation of church and state. Luther said that government should <u>guide</u> earthly matters, but that God should guide spiritual matters. He taught that everyone should have <u>freedom of conscience</u> – that people everywhere should have the right to choose their faith. He said that the state should not be involved in religious matters.

Other reformers agreed with Luther. John Calvin (1509-64) in Switzerland wrote a series of books called *The Institutes of the Christian Religion*. Like Luther, Calvin wrote about many matters of life, including separation of church and state. In the last pages of his *Institutes*, Calvin wrote that people have the right and responsibility to disobey a governmental leader if that leader goes against God's commands. He showed from the Bible that if political leaders made ungodly rules, they should be disobeyed. This teaching caused many debates over the next two centuries. In 1535 King Henry VIII of England <u>executed</u> Thomas More, his senior advisor and scholar. More disapproved of the king's actions. He said that people must be "the king's good citizens, but the Lord's first."

> *Humans are equal because the Bible says they are all made in God's image.*

The Reformation continued to spread to other countries. Many more Protestant (or "protesting") groups started in these countries, such as Lutherans in Germany, Huguenots in France, and Presbyterians in other countries like Scotland. One group in England called themselves "Puritans," meaning "ones that purify." They wanted to stay in the Church of England, the national church, and make changes in it.

All of these groups had leaders who taught similar things such as individual responsibility to God, freedom of conscience, and the **equality** of all human beings. Humans are equal because the Bible says they are all made in God's image. This teaching raised the value of people as **individuals** in people's thinking.

In those days many European societies were divided into two groups. One was a permanent upper class of landowners called "nobles" or "the nobility." The rest were the lower class called "commoners." Kings were members of the nobility and ruled by "divine right," the idea that God chose who should be king. Therefore, a king could do whatever he wanted to do. Sometimes kings would be unfair and treat people badly. Kings said their desires and commands were the law. Protestants disagreed. They said that upper and lower classes of people were **equal**, and that laws came from God.

Equality is closely connected to **individualism**. Samuel Rutherford (1600-61) was a Scottish Presbyterian minister. He wrote a book in 1644 called *Lex Rex*, meaning "the law is king." He used ideas from both Catholic and Protestant writers. In his book Rutherford said that kings, nobles and common people were all human beings. There-fore, their <u>humanity</u> makes them **equal** as **individuals**. Thus the king was not above God's law, but must obey it like everyone else. By this time most people in England believed in **equality**. However, kings and nobles still ruled the government. A civil war in 1649 removed King Charles I, but the <u>monarchy</u> was restored about 50 years later. Thus kings ruled the British Empire all through the 1700's.

These were times of great changes in Europe – changes in thinking and behavior. Merchants and other commoners already wanted more influence in society. They began to **compete** against the nobles for power in society and government. They understood that an **individual's** work made a big difference in his own well-being. People wanted a better **future** with more **materialistic** ben-efits.

By the 18th Century the British Colonies in North America were the home of those who believed in freedom, **individualism** and **equality**. This began earlier in 1620 when the Pilgrims [see Thanks-giving] wrote the *Mayflower Compact*. In that paper they said they would willingly "combine ourselves together" to live under "just and **equal** laws . . ." The Puritans arrived after the Pilgrims. They said people should be free but responsible for themselves. They taught **individual** rights, God's law and **equality**. The new land gave them opportunities for **personal improvement**. Their famous "work <u>ethic</u>" was a rule that all work should be done as if they worked for God. Their **future orientation** was clear – they believed God's forgiveness would allow them into heaven after they died. They also believed in resisting government <u>tyranny</u> as John Calvin taught. More and more colonists, who came to America over the next 150 years, believed most or all of these things. Colonial colleges such as Harvard taught these ideas to the colonies' future leaders.

This teaching in colonial schools did not make the English happy. By the 1770's, people in the colonies knew that the English king would not protect them. So they organized themselves into states, and wrote these ideas into their state <u>constitutions</u>. For ex-ample, the Virginia Constitution says, "That all men are by nature **equally** free and independent . . ." Later in the US Declaration of Independence, Thomas Jefferson wrote, "We hold these truths to be <u>self-evident</u>, that all men are **created equal**."

These ideas clearly have Protestant Christian beginnings. George Bancroft (1800-1891) was the first American historian who wrote a complete history of the US. In his book, *History of the United States, From the Discovery of the American Continent*, he wrote, "The Revolution of 1776 was a Presbyterian measure. It was the natural [result] of the principles which the Presbyterianism of the Old World [taught to] her sons." The English political leaders at that time knew this was true. Rev. William Jones told King George III himself, "This has been a Presbyterian war from the beginning..." Christianity had a major part in developing America's cultural value system.

> *Christianity had a major part in developing America's cultural value system.*

The Enlightenment
(18ᵗʰ Century)

A second cause of American culture was the <u>Enlightenment</u>. This was one of the very few movements in history that named itself. Enlightenment leaders were mostly thinkers and writers in Europe. They thought they were more "<u>enlightened</u>" than other citizens. Their goal was to enlighten others through discussions and writing about new ideas.

The main point of this movement was using <u>logic</u> and human intelligence to discover truth to build a better world. Scientific discoveries made some people think that the human mind had no limits. Some Enlightenment leaders believed human reason was superior to anything else because man was God's greatest creation. However, later leaders of the movement had no need for religion. They had <u>secular</u> reasons for teaching others. Regardless of their purposes, they all believed that the **future** was good. It would bring **improvements to their lives** if they committed themselves to make progress in society through **change**. Life would be a continual process of discovery and learning, helped by human intelligence.

This attention to the **future** meant that old traditions should be rejected. Therefore Enlightenment thinkers wanted to destroy two important authorities in society — the government and the Roman

Catholic Church. Both of these institutions had existed since the Middle Ages (500 – 1500 AD) and represented the old ways of the past. But the movement took different forms in England and France.

In France the Enlightenment became very anti-Christian. The Catholic Church earlier had removed most Protestants from the country. The church and government had total control of society. So the Enlightenment thinkers attacked the authority of both of them. Their three main goals – liberty, **equality**, and brotherhood for all – all came from Christianity. But French thinkers did not use the Bible when they wanted to improve society. They developed their own idea of what was right and wrong. They believed people who disagreed with them were enemies who should be killed. Thus many thousands of innocent people died in the French Revolution (1789-1799). It caused many <u>riots</u> in Paris and other French cities. Everywhere in France people were afraid of being punished, <u>tortured</u> and executed. The revolution ended when one of their army's generals, Napoleon Bonaparte (1769-1821), became the French <u>dictator</u>.

The Enlightenment was different in England. Many Christians were active in government and made it more open to **change** and new ideas. Famous thinkers such as Francis Bacon, Isaac Newton and John Locke taught ideas found in the Bible. They believed reason and logic should be used when studying the Bible. They made changes in the government slowly, not quickly as they were made in France.

Colonists brought this kind of enlightenment to North America. Therefore, the goal of the earliest schools of higher education in the colonies (Harvard, Yale, Princeton, etc.) was to create educated church leaders for the people. This remained true until the American Revolutionary War (1775-1783) was over. In fact, the American Revolution was the result of the best Enlightenment ideas related to politics. At the end of the 18th Century Enlightenment thinkers in the US rejected Christian teaching as the French had earlier.

The Enlightenment added several ideas that became part of American culture. **Individualism** was one. Another was the **positive nature of change** – the idea that things can and will be better when we work hard and use our minds. New scientific discoveries also created a hopefulness for the **future**. The thinking was, "The past is history; long live the future!" Finally, the Enlightenment's concept of **equality** was very similar to what the Bible said, but had less religious importance to it.

The Industrial Revolution
(18th & 19th Centuries)

A third source of cultural values in America was the Industrial Revolution. Many of the new ideas from the Reformation and the Enlightenment changed people's thinking in many ways. A change of thinking normally produces a change in behavior and society. This change encouraged people to be creative. Western society has never been the same since the Industrial Revolution first began in England and quickly spread to America.

Before the Industrial Revolution craftsmen made most goods by hand in homes or in workshops with small machines. To increase production, merchants had to hire workers and provide houses for them too. Merchants also had to train young workers with no experience (called "apprentices"). Sometimes workers were hired by more than one merchant. All of these things and other problems increased the cost of making goods. It was impossible for the merchant to make goods that cost less. They needed a big change in the way goods were made.

By the middle of the 1700's England had become the world's most important colonial power. English colonies provided raw materials and new trading partners for Great Britain. In return people in the colonies needed more products. Thus the demand for goods increased quickly. This greater demand for goods caused prices to increase. If prices were too high, the amount of sales would go down because goods cost too much. Therefore English merchants had to find cheaper ways to produce goods quickly. They also had to sell their goods at lower prices than other merchants. For that reason **competition** became an important part of the British economy.

In the 1730's changes began to occur in England's textile industry. Cotton first needed to have the seeds removed after it was picked. Then the cotton had to be spun into thread. Next the thread was woven into fabric. It took a long time and many different steps. In the middle of the 1700's several new inventions greatly reduced the time it took to make fabric. For example, the steam engine meant that more work could be done faster and with fewer workers.

Steam engines were made of iron and used coal to burn. England had a lot of coal and iron. This helped produce more steam engines. These steam-powered machines also made changes in farming, transportation and other industries.

This need to make more goods faster and cheaper spread to the British colonies in North America. After Eli Whitney (1765-1825) attended Yale College, he invented the cotton 'gin' (short for *engine*) in 1793. This machine removed the seeds from cotton and greatly reduced the time it took to make cotton into fabric. Robert Fulton (1765-1815) was the first American to build a steam-powered engine for boats. Steamboats quickly became common in North American rivers and greatly improved transportation in the US. Francis Cabot Lowell (1775-1817) built the first cotton mill that manufactured textiles completely by machines in the early 1800's. Whitney is also an important person because he was the first person to use <u>mass-production</u> to make a product − guns. Other people made similar inventions that saved time and reduced costs of making all kinds of goods.

All of these changes affected Americans' thinking and behavior. They believed they could have greater **control over the environment** and increase production of many kinds of goods. For example, by 1776 nearly one-third of all of British ships were built in North America. Americans also began to think about life in economic terms. Machines had to be **practical** to meet certain needs. They also had to be **efficient** − they had to cost less to run than paying workers to produce the same amount of goods. Factory owners and businessmen quickly learned the importance of the **bottom line** − "How much will it cost?" and "How long will it take?" Public demand and **competition** against other factories made **control over time** an important factor in production.

The Industrial Revolution rapidly increased the size of the upper and middle classes of American society. These were the people who received the profits from successful factories. Wealthy people enjoyed this <u>prosperity</u> and became more **materialistic**, measuring their success by the amount of things they bought and owned. But many of them used their wealth to help society by building hospitals and libraries and improving education. This was true in England too. For example, before the Industrial Revolution Britain had only two universities, Oxford and Cambridge. Afterwards, new schools offering all kinds of training programs were created.

Materialism also reached the working and lower classes. Products and goods were more available and affordable for most people. Freedom to move, **individualism** and hard work made the new "American Dream" possible. This dream included a good-paying job, owning one's home and car(s), getting a college education and a having a comfortable life for oneself and one's family. Philosopher and historian Henry Adams (1838-1918) wrote in *History of the United States* that the original "American Dream" was that the American people would limit the size and control of the government. But the economy continued to grow and Europe was at peace. Thus people began thinking the "American Dream" was an economic and **materialistic** opportunity, not a political one.

Over the years, a **"doing" orientation** developed. People began to feel important and valuable more from their job (company manager, businessman, sales representative, etc.) than from their family relationships. This change in identity slowly replaced the older British (and non-Western) "being" orientation. It became more clear in the middle to late 1800's, between the Civil War (1861-65) and World War I (1914-17). During this time American society went through its deepest change. Many people moved westward and bought unsettled land. This created national <u>markets</u> for goods and services. New <u>technologies</u> in transportation, communication and industry created larger companies and businesses. The growth of bigger companies required changes in banking, steel, oil and insurance companies. It also created the need for managers and bureaucrats, which strengthened the **"doing"** or **work orientation** and made it a permanent part of North American culture.

The Western Movement
(called "Manifest Destiny")
(17ᵗʰ through 19th Centuries)

The last source that helped develop cultural values in the US was the American Westward Movement. This is defined as the movement westward to settle the rest of the North American continent. Generally speaking, settling of all of North America was a westward movement. Europeans came from the east and first settled on the East Coast. There was no way to expand their colonies except to move west.

The movement across the whole continent came in several stages. The goal of the first stage was to settle the <u>coastline</u>. By 1670 pioneers had settled all the coastal lowlands, as far as boats could travel on rivers inland, except along the coast of Florida. The frontier line – that unseen line that separated "settled" and "unsettled" land – lay at the edge of the highland area that leads to the Appalachian Mountains.

The colonist William Penn (1644-1718) granted freedom to everyone who came to his colony. Thus, many European immigrants who were unhappy in their native country quickly settled in Pennsylvania in the early 1700's. Other settlers during this time moved westward into the valleys of the Appalachians. Some, like Daniel Boone (1734-1820), went beyond the mountains. He led pioneers through the <u>Cumberland Gap</u> into Kentucky in 1775 along a trail called the "Wilderness Road." This is why some colonies claimed land west of the Appalachians before the Revolutionary War began the next year.

During this time colonists developed different attitudes depending on where they lived. Frontier people lived **independently** and didn't trust people living in eastern cities. People in the cities thought pioneers in the west were rude and uncivilized. People who lived in the frontier had to think for themselves and be creative. **Self-help** was important for them to survive hard conditions. They built log cabins and big barns, and wore animal skins for clothing.

The frontier line moved even farther west after the Revolutionary War. The US added the Northwest Territory in a <u>treaty</u> with Britain in 1794. This is generally the Ohio Valley and Great Lakes area. At that time the natural western boundary of the States was the Mississippi River. Ohio became a state in 1803; that same year President Thomas Jefferson (1743-1826) bought the area called the Louisiana Purchase from France. This one purchase did two things. First, it gave the US twice as much territory as it had before. Second, it pushed the frontier line west of the Mississippi River. The areas of Florida (1821), Texas (1836), Oregon (1846), California (1848), the Southwest (1848), the Rocky Mountain and Great Plains areas were added until the frontier disappeared. In fact, one government official declared in 1890 that a frontier no longer separated settled and unsettled land.

In 1845 this process of settling the whole continent became known as "Manifest Destiny" (meaning "known future" or "the future is obvious"). Newspaper editor John L. O'Sullivan wrote, "our manifest destiny [is] to [occupy] the continent [given] by <u>Providence</u> for the free development of our yearly multiplying millions." But this idea was not new. Rev. Samuel West, a Boston minister, said 70 years earlier in 1775, "I cannot help hoping, even believing, that Providence has designed this continent . . . to be the [safe place] of liberty and true religion." The next year patriot John Adams (1735-1826) signed the Declaration of Independence. Afterwards he wrote to his wife that he expected the Fourth of July holiday would be celebrated "from one end of the continent to the other." Thus from the beginnings of US history, a nation spreading across all of North America was part of the popular thinking.

This idea tied together all of the cultural values that make America different. It also helped Americans believe they were different. Life on the frontier and in the west made tough **individualism** a valuable quality. Settlers had to be **self-sufficient**, since the government services were not available until many years later. Life centered on the **work** to be done. They needed to settle the land to **control the environment** and **improve their lives**. Tools and new inventions from the Industrial Revolution (see previous section) had to be **efficient** and **practical** or people would not buy them. People who owned land had to work hard to bring **change**, which would increase their **material possessions**.

The frontier made everyone – settlers, pioneers, and later cowboys – **equal** in position and rank. All of them started with the same kind of unsettled land. Life was simple but hard. Thus **informality** became a normal pattern of behavior. It had started earlier with the colonists' dislike for the idea of the nobility. The image of the tough western cowboy continued that idea. Communication was **direct, open** and <u>blunt</u>. Freedom to pursue the "American Dream" became the common factor among most of them, which strengthened the idea that everyone was **equal**.

The 21st Century

Since **change** is an important value in the States, Americans expect changes to occur. Progress in technology shows that changes do bring some improvements. This thinking creates opportunities for people to make even more changes in society. Thus the United States has been the birthplace of a wide variety of ideas, groups and movements. For example, a visitor will find a large variety of churches in the States, each with different teachings.

Major changes occurred in the US in the 1960's. A huge number of children were born after World War 2 (between 1946-1964). That generation is called the "Baby Boom" Generation (also called "Boomers"). This large number of children increased the need for **competition**. Improvements in communication also helped popular culture become widespread. New ideas reached larger numbers of people faster. Parents raised this new generation differently from any generation before it.

Boomers grew up and entered adult life beginning in the 1960's. Many of them rejected the traditional ideas of their parents, especially religion. They were going to do things their own way. Many accepted ideas that were different from some of the values described earlier. A few Boomers tried to make changes violently. Others led protests and rallies at colleges and universities.

Many of the changes that Boomers wanted to make did not happen immediately. But as they got older and became leaders in society, changes did occur – in government policies, law, medicine, education, the arts, and in ideas and values. When people visit the US today, they find a strange mixture of both old and new ideas. A few of these new ideas are described below.

Relativism

The first new idea is **relativism**. It came from several sources. It says that nothing is absolute, perfect and unchanging. Everything changes and will continue to change. This idea seems to fit well into the list of American values, since **change** is already one of them. But relativism takes a big step away from traditional American thinking. For example, many Protestant Christians in America believe that God and the Bible are absolute and true. Relativism denies these beliefs.

Another example is the idea of the university. The word *university* comes from two Greek words — *uni* meaning "one," and *verse* originally meaning "to turn." Together they mean that wherever people examined or studied things in the world, they could find a unity that came from God the Creator. In other words, everything in the universe had design, meaning and purpose. These were absolute. Science and research could confirm that some values were universal and true for everyone.

Philosophers were the first to replace these absolutes with relativism. Then artists and entertainers promoted relativism. Professors at colleges and universities later taught relativism to their students. Much of American society now accepts relativism.

—— *Multiculturalism* ——

The second idea is called **diversity** or **multiculturalism**. These words mean that all ideas are equally reasonable, equally acceptable and have equal value. It is not important where ideas come from. The fact that people believe different ideas is what makes the ideas valuable, important and equal, not the ideas themselves.

—— *Tolerance* ——

Another idea that has become common since the 1960's is **tolerance**. In earlier days tolerance meant that people should simply allow or permit beliefs different from their own. It now means that almost any idea can be promoted in society. American society now encourages citizens to accept as equals other people with different beliefs and values, regardless of what they are. People who disagree with this new tolerance are called "intolerant." In its strongest form tolerance means that it is wrong for people to change the beliefs of others.

These newer ideas sound fair and reasonable. They appear to promote acceptance and a feeling of harmony. However, for a culture or country to survive, people must agree on what is true, good and beautiful. They must choose what is important and valuable to them as a group. A country or group cannot exist if it accepts all ideas equally or shares no common ideas other than ones like relativism, multiculturalism and tolerance.

A country or group cannot exist if it accepts all ideas equally or shares no common ideas other than ones like relativism, multiculturalism and tolerance.

Throughout history every culture has had a creation story. This story tells the beginning and early history of society. It also states which ideas and values are important. These ideas form the foundation of society. Each generation teaches their cultural values to the next generation. This is what keeps a cultural group of people living and working together as a society.

America's creation story has three parts to it: *the Pilgrims, the Puritans* , and *the American Revolution* [see Independence Day]. Christianity clearly influenced all three. American people are the most religious of any Western country. Part of the Pledge of Allegiance says, "One nation under God . . ." America is the only country in the world that has "God" printed on its money: "In God we trust," which is the national <u>motto</u>. The US government pays ministers to serve in the military. (These ministers in the military are called 'chaplains'.) Many of the famous government buildings in Washington, DC, have verses from the Bible on them.

The ideas of relativism, multiculturalism and tolerance have not mixed well with the older, traditional American values. They ignore the main values of America's creation story that have held society together for over 200 years. Thus problems and confusion now exist in America. Some people believe the older values should be <u>emphasized</u>. They also reject these newer ideas. Other Americans believe the new ideas should replace the old ones.

Conclusion

When people visit the US, they will discover many things about Americans. They will find that most Americans are surrounded by and depend on new technology – things like computers, cell phones, the Internet, etc. These tools save **time**. When they don't work, Americans quickly become unhappy. People in the States are also busy – very busy, probably too busy. Most appear to be friendly. The average American knows a lot of people but few have deep friendships. One reason for this is that they frequently move from one place or state to another. Americans love their privacy and their "space." They see almost everything in life as an **individual** right. Generally, they like sports, hobbies, games, entertainment and other forms of recreation. Hospitality is not a high value for most of them. They save very little money, and are usually concerned about the economy.

The most obvious American value, and the one they believe is as important as **individualism**, is **equality**. Alexis de Tocqueville (1805-59) was a French political philosopher and researcher. His government sent him to the States to study American prisons in 1831. He also studied American politics and government, society, religion and customs. Four years later his research was published as a book, *Democracy in America*. It remains the most complete study ever done on life in America. In it he said,

> . . [T]he gradual development of the principle of equality is a providential fact . . . it is universal, it is <u>durable</u>, it constantly [stays away from] all human <u>interference</u> . .

Tocqueville was very pleased by what he saw in America. He wrote,

> Where else could we find greater causes of hope, or more instructive lessons? Let us look to America . . . [T]hose principles on which the American [structures] rest, those   principles of order, of the balance of powers, of true liberty, of deep and sincere respect for right, are [required for] all <u>republics</u>; they ought to be common to all.

But he was not blind to what could happen in the future. Later he warned that too much **individualism** would weaken society and make it lose its unity if people forgot its creation story. Some observers say 21st Century American society has been weak for many years because it has lost its most important values.

> *Too much individualism would weaken society and make it lose its unity if people forgot its creation story.*

Probably the best way to experience American culture is to get to know a number of Americans who come from different backgrounds and have different beliefs and experiences. That is what the "American experiment" is all about – having the freedom to learn from others, to explore the many ideas and issues of our time. But you must have courage, ask questions and be diligent. It may take some time before you find Americans who are able to become your friend. You may need to try several times to find good American friends. But they are there if you look hard enough. In the United States you can find people who believe almost anything. Good, bad, strange or different, you can find it in the USA.

Vocabulary

*Baby Boom Generation *(noun)* – American children born
    between 1946-1964.

blunt *(adjective)* – direct, sometimes unfriendly in manner.

coastline *(noun)* – the land along the ocean.

constitution *(noun)* – the written principles and rules, governing
    a country.

*craftsman *(noun)* – a man who makes things with skill by his
    hands.

Cumberland Gap *(noun)* – a narrow path in the Cumberland
    Mountains in Kentucky.

diligent *(adjective)* – hardworking.

dictator *(noun)* – a ruler with total power.

durable *(adjective)* – long wearing, long lasting.

emphasize *(verb)* – to place importance on.

*Enlightenment *(noun)* – a movement in philosophy in the 18th
    Century that put attention on human reason and progress.

*enlightened *(adjective)* – in the condition of understanding; to
    have knowledge.

ethic *(noun)* – moral or correct behavior.

execute *(verb)* – to kill, especially by government or military.

fabric *(noun)* – cloth material.

*freedom of conscience *(noun)* – having the power to think and
    make choices without being stopped.

guide *(verb)* – to direct

hire *(verb)* – to pay someone to do something, employ.

humanity *(noun)* – the state or condition of being human.

immigrant *(noun)* – a person who moves to another
    country to live.

*Industrial Revolution *(noun)* – a movement in the 17th and 18th
    Centuries when goods changed from being made at home
    or the workshop to being made in factories by machines.

*interference *(noun)* – something that stops a situation or
    discussion, usually without permission.

issue *(noun)* – a matter of concern.

Vocabulary

logic *(noun)* – a system of reasoning.

market *(noun)* – a place or store that sells things.

*****mass-production** *(noun)* – the process of manufacturing or growing a large amount of a product at one time.

monarchy *(noun)* – a government run by a king or queen (monarch) usually with limited powers.

motto *(noun)* – a short saying that states the basic belief of a nation, organization, etc.

pioneer *(noun)* – one of the first people to enter new land to live and work there.

*****prosperity** *(noun)* – the state of being successful and wealthy.

*****Protestant Reformation** *(noun)* – a religious movement in the 16th Century that rejected or changed many Roman Catholic teachings and resulted in establishing Protestant churches.

*****protocol** *(noun)* – rules of behavior and conduct, customs, manners.

*****Providence** *(noun)* – a name for God (the God who provides and cares for people).

raw *(adjective)* – in a natural state, not yet manufactured.

republic *(noun)* – a form of government in which citizens vote for people to represent them and to make laws.

riot *(noun)* – an act of violent behavior by a large group.

*****secular** *(adjective)* – relating to this world without God.

*****self-evident** *(adjective)* – quickly obvious or clear.

support *(verb)* – to provide the money for necessities of life.

technology *(noun)* – science and theoretical engineering used in practical applications.

textile *(noun)* – cloth, fabric made by weaving.

torture *(verb)* – to abuse physically and cause great pain.

treaty *(noun)* – a formal agreement between nations.

*****tyranny** *(noun)* – terror and force used by a government to rule people.

weaken *(verb)* – to make or become less strong.

Exploring

America's Holidays

Party!

Holiday (HOL- i- day):

1. A day on which custom or the law dictates a halting of general business activity to commemorate or celebrate a particular event. 2. A religious feast day; a holy day. 3. A day free from work that one may spend at leisure; a day off.

-American Heritage Dictionary

*Underlined words have definitions at the end of each holiday that are provided by *The Basic Newbury House Dictionary.*
Definitions with an asterisk (*) are supplied by the author.

Labor Day

Labor Day respects working people of all kinds and their different jobs. People in the US, Puerto Rico and Canada celebrate it on the first Monday in September. Labor Day means that the summer season has ended.

The history of Labor Day starts in the 1700's. At that time factories made many <u>products</u> cheaper and faster that those made at home by hand. People quickly learned that work in factories was different from work at home. They worked for longer hours. Many factories were dirty and unsafe. Even young children worked in factories. Many factory workers wanted to improve the place where they worked. Thus in the 1800's they created groups of workers called <u>unions</u>.

The idea of a holiday for workers developed slowly. Two factory workers, Matthew Maguire from Paterson, NJ, and Peter J. McGuire from New York City, organized the first workers' day parade in New York City in September 1882. In later years, more working people liked the idea of a holiday that recognized them and their work. They wanted the government to call it "Labor Day." In 1887 Oregon became the first state to make Labor Day an <u>official</u> holiday. One by one other states made the same holiday for their workers.

Labor ★★ Day ★★★★★★ first Monday in September

However, Labor Day was not yet a national holiday. In 1894 workers for the Pullman Railroad Company stopped working. The company did not agree to improvements the workers wanted. This is called a <u>strike</u> against the company. It caused many problems for people around the country. One problem was that some US mail was not being delivered. Then a court ruled that the workers must return to work.

President Grover Cleveland then sent soldiers to help stop the strike. Many Americans agreed with the President, but people in unions were angry with him. Therefore he made Labor Day a national holiday in the US to help make peace with the workers.

Today some unions have Labor Day activities, but there is no national custom for this holiday. Since Labor Day is on a Monday, it makes a three-day-weekend. Since this weekend comes at the end of summer, many Americans go on a short trip and go camping, fishing, or visiting other parts of the country. Others have picnics, play sports and games, or do other outdoor activities.

Sometimes you may hear Americans speak badly about their jobs, but most are probably glad to have their jobs. They know their paycheck provides the money they need to have a comfortable life.

Many American holidays and customs come from traditions in the Bible. The idea of a weekend is one example. In the Bible God made one day a week to be a day of rest. For Jews that day is Saturday; for Christians it is Sunday. Most people from these faiths try not to work on these two days. They attend church services and worship God and rest. That is how the weekend in America began. Labor Day gives one day off from work each year; the weekend gives one day off each week.

Vocabulary

official *(adjective)* – of or related to a position of power or authority.

paycheck *(noun)* – a salary or wage check.

product *(noun)* – anything that is manufactured or grown to be sold.

strike *(noun)* – a work stoppage because of disagreements with management.

*three-day-weekend *(noun)* – Saturday, Sunday and Monday when Monday is a holiday.

union *(noun)* – an organization of workers.

weekend *(noun)* – Saturday and Sunday.

Columbus Day

Columbus Day is the holiday named for the famous Italian explorer, Christopher Columbus. This holiday occurs on October 12th, the date he found land that was called the "New World." The US celebration is the second Monday in October. However, many South American countries celebrate it on October 12th.

Christopher and his family came from Genoa, Italy. In the Italian language his name is "Colombo." *Columbus* is the English name. He was born in the city of Genoa in 1451, the first of five children. His two brothers, Bartholomew and Diego, worked with Christopher making maps. Christopher wanted to travel across the ocean. He had little education, but he learned Spanish and taught himself Latin. He also learned about sailing on short trips in the ocean.

When Christopher was born, many people thought that the earth was flat. But educated people slowly started to believe the earth was round. Columbus wanted to sail across the ocean to show that sailing to the west would take him to the east. In his personal <u>journal</u> he wrote:

> *It was the Lord who put into my mind (I could feel his hand upon me) the fact that it would be possible to sail [west] from here to the [East] Indies. All who heard of my project laughed . . . There is no question that the <u>inspiration</u> was from [God], because He comforted me with. . . inspiration from the Holy Scriptures [Bible].*

Columbus
Day

October 12th

However, Columbus had another reason to sail across the sea. As he read the Bible, he found parts, such as the Old Testament book of Isaiah, chapter 49, that said,

> *Listen to me, you islands, and hear this, you distant nations: Before I was born the Lord called me; from my birth he [spoke] my name . . . I will also make you a light for the [foreign nations], that you may bring my <u>salvation</u> to the ends of the earth" (verses 1,6).*

33

Columbus thought these verses spoke about him personally. In fact, the name *Christopher* means "Christ-bearer," or "one who brings the message of Christ." So he believed that God wanted him to sail to the "ends of the earth" with God's message of salvation.

Traveling by sea was dangerous and cost a lot of money in those days. Columbus needed money to sail to the East Indies. The kings of Portugal and England would not help him. After some time, King Ferdinand and Queen Isabella of Spain agreed to help this man from Genoa. They gave him enough money for his trip.

On August 3, 1492 Columbus sailed west across the Atlantic Ocean. Three new ships, the *Pinta, Nina,* and *Santa Maria,* carried him and 90 men. In his journal of this trip, he wrote, "For the . . . journey I did not make use of <u>intelligence</u>, <u>mathematics</u> or maps. It is simply . . . what Isaiah had [said] . . ." Columbus really believed God was guiding him across the waters of the Atlantic.

After five weeks of sailing westward, his men became worried and afraid. They sailed farther than anyone had sailed before. They had not seen any land for over three weeks and wanted to return to Spain. Columbus asked them to keep sailing only three more days. If they saw no land in three days, then they would turn around and go home. Two days later on October 12th at 2:00 AM they saw land. Later that morning, Columbus and some of his men got in a smaller boat and went to an island of the Bahamas. He named the island *San Salvador,* meaning "holy Savior." He got down on his knees and kissed the beach. He also put a cross in the sand for "Jesus Christ our Lord and in honor of the Christian faith." Then Columbus prayed,

Columbus Day

observed second Monday in October

O Lord Almighty and everlasting God, by your Holy Word you have created the heaven and the earth, and the sea . . . [You] have [used] us, your humble servants, that your holy Name may be <u>proclaimed</u> in this part of the earth.

Columbus really wanted to obey God on his trips, but he made poor choices when dealing with problems. The <u>sailors</u> became unhappy when they found very little gold. Later on this trip he caught some <u>Native Americans</u>. He called them "Indians" because he thought he was near India. He took them back to Spain. His second and third trips had many problems including angry natives, a failed <u>colony</u>, sinking ships, and sailors dying. As a result he became less popular back in Spain.

His fourth and last voyage began in 1502 and was his happiest. He brought his 13-year-old son Ferdinand and many older boys with him. Columbus said they worked better and were easier to control than the older men. When he sailed to an area now called Panama, natives told him of another great ocean – the Pacific – but he never saw it. This final trip took him two-and-one-half years because he was unable to leave Jamaica for one year. By the time he returned to Spain, Queen Isabella had died, and King Ferdinand did not want to see him. At 53 years old, he was tired and very weak. He died on May 20, 1506. With him were his two sons, some faithful servants and a few close friends.

When Columbus arrived in South America (Venezuela), he wrote in his journal, "I believe that this is a very great continent which until today has been unknown." He died thinking that he had been somewhere south of China. He never knew that he had discovered a new area of the world and was the first European who arrived there. People did not clearly understand the sailing route to the East Indies until another explorer sailed around the world 16 years later.

Most people remember Columbus as an important explorer. But Columbus thought of himself as both an explorer and a missionary. He also wrote in his journal about his first trip, "I hope in our Lord that it will be the greatest honor to Christianity that, unexpectedly, has ever come about."

The name "America" came from the explorer, Amerigo Vespucci, who said he discovered the "new world" in 1497. Columbus never debated this point because he thought he discovered the East Indies. In 1507 someone said that the new area should be named after Vespucci, because people said, "Amerigo discovered it." This name quickly became popular, but later Vespucci's claim was shown to be false. The Republic of Colombia, however, is named after Columbus, as are many rivers, boats, cities, buildings, streets, and other things.

Columbus Day

October 12th

Columbus Day was first celebrated in New York City in 1792, 300 years after the discovery. 100 years later US President Benjamin Harrison led the celebration on the holiday's 400th anniversary. In 1992 the 500th anniversary was celebrated all around the world. Columbus Day has been celebrated each year in the US since 1920. In the States there are no customs related to the holiday, but events include parades, speeches and outdoor water activities such as sailing races. The holiday is a more important event in South America.

Vocabulary

anniversary *(noun)* – one or more years after the date on which an event took place.

claim *(noun)* – a demand for something that one has a right to.

colony *(noun)* – a group of people who have moved to another area, but are still governed by their home country.

debate *(verb)* – to consider, to discuss.

***East Indies** *(noun)* – the southern part of Asia from India to Indonesia.

inspiration *(noun)* – someone or something that makes a person work hard or gives them new ideas.

intelligence *(noun)* – the ability to learn, understand, and use information.

journal *(noun)* – a written record of the day's events or one's thoughts and feelings.

mathematics *(noun)* – the study of numbers, symbols, and forms that follow strict rules and laws.

***Native American** *(noun)* – American Indians.

***proclaim** *(verb)* – to declare or announce publicly through speech or writing.

route *(noun)* – a path along which one travels.

sailor *(noun)* – a person who works on a ship.

***salvation** *(noun)* – the freedom from the power and effects of sin that God gives to people.

voyage *(noun)* – a long journey, usually by water.

Halloween

Over the years Halloween celebrations in America have been a time of fun for children. However, in recent years many Halloween activities have become dangerous. Halloween is a holiday that comes from several mysterious religions that joined together. Europeans brought these traditions to America. A summary about their history and customs follows.

One Halloween tradition comes from the <u>Druids</u> of England, Scotland and Ireland. The Druids were <u>priests</u> who taught a religion of many gods. One of their chief gods was named Saman (pronounced Sah WEEN). The Druids said that Saman would tell the spirits of dead people to visit the earth on October 31st, the last day of the year according to their calendar. Leaves fall in the autumn season when people prepare for winter. The Druids said that autumn was a symbol of dying, and that winter was the season of death. Therefore, they believed that the earth and the spirit world were very close to each other, especially during the night of October 31st. This date was their New Year's Eve. On that night they believed these spirits would visit people on earth.

To keep the evil spirits away from people, Druids told them to make an animal <u>sacrifice</u> on Druid <u>altars</u>. The priests used the <u>organs</u> of these dead animals to do two things. *First,* they told the future. *Second*, they helped make peace with angry evil spirits nearby. Happy spirits would leave them alone. Later the dead animals were burned in "bonefires," or <u>bonfires</u>. The priests told the people that fires scare away evil spirits that didn't like all the light coming from the flames.

Halloween

October 31st

Other customs began over the years. If the spirits caused no problems for a family, that family celebrated later that night. Parents sent the children out to collect food from friends and neighbors. To help them stay away from evil spirits, parents dressed up the children as <u>ghosts</u> and other figures that looked like evil spirits, trying to scare away the real spirits! As children were outside, they heard what people said the evil spirits were doing – kicking over garbage cans, taking gates off fences, letting farm animals loose and spilling paint on houses. So they began doing these things themselves. They would visit a house and call out, _Trick or Treat!_ If they did not receive what they wanted (a treat), they would cause problems for that family (the trick). Some families cut out <u>scary</u> faces in large <u>turnips</u> and put them around the edge of their property. They thought this would help keep evil spirits away.

Another event was "<u>bobbing</u>" for apples. People thought the apple was a sign of protection. They would bring a large <u>bucket</u> into their home, fill it with water, and put the apples into the water. Then one by one, each person would try to pick up the floating apples using only their teeth. They believed that those who got an apple with their teeth were safe from the evil spirits that night.

American Halloween customs also came from Central Europe. Hundreds of years ago many people there believed in <u>witchcraft</u>, a religion of evil power. This is also called <u>Black Magic</u>. <u>Witches</u> (females) and <u>warlocks</u> (males) usually wore black clothing and acted like priests for the Devil. In the Bible the Devil is God's enemy and the center of all evil in the world. Black represents darkness and death to these priests. People were very afraid of witches and warlocks because they talked with the Devil and used his power. They believed these evil priests could change themselves into black cats, bats and spiders. They also thought witches could fly on <u>brooms</u>.

Halloween

October 31st

Witches have several days of the year that are their special religious days. One of them is May 1st, a day called May Day in many countries. The last special day of the calendar year for witches is October 31st. They believe that any <u>spell</u> they had made earlier in the year that had not yet occurred would occur that night. Because of this, witches and warlocks celebrate on this day with feasts and noisy partying. Part of the celebration is cutting out <u>pumpkins</u> with scary faces that look like the evil spirits they contact.

Halloween celebrations also have a connection to the Roman Catholic Church (RCC). It seems the Church wanted to change the holiday, not add to its tradition. One Catholic Church practice, praying to or with dead "saints," seems to be similar to Halloween's attention to the spirits of dead people. The RCC says "saints" are persons who were chosen by the church to be honored after their death because of their good works. Many of the early saints were killed because of their faith. The Pope, leader of the RCC, chose dates that would be named for their saints. After many centuries, the number of RCC saints grew very large. There were saints for safe travel, financial success, healing, children, families, etc. The calendar did not have enough days to honor all of them. So someone suggested the idea of an "All Saints Day," a day when all saints could be honored.

The church first celebrated All Saints Day in the springtime. Then in 732 AD Pope Gregory III moved the holiday to November 1st. They called it "Allhallowmas" *(All* = every; *hallow* = saint; *mas* = RCC worship service, called a "mass"). *The* RCC then told their members they could begin celebrating All Saints Day the night before November 1st. The name of the service therefore was changed. The "all" was dropped, the "mas" was changed to "een" (a shorter form of the word "evening"), and it became *Halloween* (meaning "saints' evening"). Church members attended this service and prayed to or with their favorite saints to help them in their prayers. This change in the Catholic holiday caused their members to think more about dead saints on the very same night that others were celebrating evil spirits and powers!

The real question is, *Why did Pope Gregory III move Allhallowmas to November 1st, and then change it to October 31st?* He probably did this to stop people from celebrating evil and death and to start honoring saints in a special church service. Many people think this change did not help. People became more interested in the evil celebrations because RCC members were going out to church services that night when evil activities were happening.

Halloween

October 31st

Another important event occurred on October 31st. On that date in 1517 AD, a Roman Catholic priest named Martin Luther nailed a list of 95 complaints on the door of the Wittenberg Church in Germany. After studying the Bible for several years, he believed that the RCC was teaching many things that were different from what he read in the Bible. A short time later he left the church and started a movement called the Reformation, trying to change the RCC. Luther wanted to correct the Church's teaching and practice. This created the <u>Protestant</u> part of <u>Christendom</u>. Those who joined Luther believed the Bible was the authority over the church. Catholics believed Protestants turned away from their faith and church.

Traditional Halloween activities still include <u>haunted</u> houses, bobbing for apples, and children going "trick-or-treating" – when they dress up as ghosts, monsters, animals, etc., and ask for candy from their neighbors. Traditional colors for Halloween are orange and black. Many churches have different activities on Halloween night. They replace witches, Black Magic and other evil themes with <u>costume</u> parties, harvest festivals or activities with Christian themes that are safer for kids. They usually include candy, games, contests, and other fun things to do for children and families.

Vocabulary

altar *(noun)* – a high flat surface like a table, for religious ceremonies.

***black magic** *(noun)* – witchcraft; the practice or use of power believed to come from evil supernatural sources to change events or people.

***bob** *(verb)* – to move up and down quickly.

bonfire *(noun)* – a large fire made outside.

broom *(noun)* – a cleaning tool made of long, stiff threads (bristles) attached to a handle.

bucket *(noun)* – a round container with an open top.

***Christendom** *(noun)* – that part of the world where Christianity is the main religion.

complaint *(noun)* – an expression of unhappiness or annoyance about something.

costume *(noun)* – a style of clothes worn especially by an actor or for entertainment.

Druids *(noun)* – priests in a very old non-Christian religion in Great Britain.

ghost *(noun)* – the spirit of a dead person.

haunted *(adjective)* – visited by ghosts.

organ *(noun)* – a part of a plant, animal or human being that has a specific purpose.

priest *(noun)* – in some Christian churches a person with the authority to conduct religious ceremonies and who is often in charge of a church.

*Protestant *(noun)* – one of the two primary parts of Christendom, the other being Catholicism.

pumpkin *(noun)* – a large orange fruit with a hard outside shell and soft insides.

*Reformation *(noun)* – a religious movement in the 16th Century that rejected or changed many Roman Catholic teachings and resulted in establishing Protestant churches.

sacrifice *(noun)* – an offering to a god.

saint *(noun)* – a person chosen by God.

scary *(adjective)* – causing fear, frightful.

spell *(noun)* – words or actions that cause a magic effect.

*trick or treat *(noun)* – a greeting that children say Halloween night when they collect candy from neighbors' homes.

turnip *(noun)* – a small vegetable with a red outside and white insides.

*warlock *(noun)* – a man who practices magic.

witch *(noun)* – a woman who practices magic.

*witchcraft *(noun)* – the use of magic, usually related to evil.

Veterans Day

Veterans Day honors everyone who has been in the United States military. It came from a holiday called Armistice Day that celebrated the end of the First World War (WW I). The word *armistice* means "peace treaty." President Woodrow Wilson in 1919 said that the armistice should be celebrated on November 11th when WW1 ended. The first Armistice Day was a day of mourning for those who died in that war.

In the years after WW I people learned more about the needs of their country's veterans. Many had returned from the war with different medical and mental problems. In 1938 Congress passed a law to help veterans. This law also made Armistice Day a national holiday. Two years later the Veterans Administration became a more important part of the government. The leader of this administration now reports directly to the President of the United States.

Then the US fought in more wars – World War II (WW II) and the Korean War. The public knew that veterans from these wars needed the same kind of help that earlier veterans received. People asked, "Should we have holidays for the ends of these wars too?" In 1954 Congress gave Armistice Day a new name – Veterans Day. This holiday would honor all veterans, not just the ones who fought in war. To make the holiday more useful to people, some states moved the celebration of the holiday to the fourth Monday in October. This created a three-day weekend [see Labor Day].

Veterans Day

VETERANS' DAY VALUES

November 11th

Normal celebrations of Veterans Day include parades with lots of American flags, speeches and other outdoor activities. At Arlington National Cemetery in Washington, DC a special ceremony is held at the

Tomb of the Unknown [Soldier]. Many people visit famous war monuments and memorials [see Memorial Day]. Veterans groups organize picnics, dances and other activities. Stores will have special sales. Many Americans use the longer weekend to go on a short trip to camp, fish, or visit friends or relatives.

Generally speaking, people of all religious faiths in America celebrate this holiday in similar ways. In many churches around the country, however, either the minister or people in church pray for the men and women in the military, and those "missing in action" – ones who never returned from battle. Pastors also may talk in churches on or before Veterans Day about military themes using parts of the Bible.

Vocabulary

ceremony *(noun)* – a formal event, usually with rituals.

Congress *(noun)* – in the USA, a governing group made up of the elected members of the House of Representatives and the Senate.

honor *(verb)* – to give praise and respect to another.

mourning *(noun)* – a traditional way of expressing sorrow for a dead person.

pastor *(noun)* – *a* minister in charge of a church.

three-day-weekend *(noun)* – Saturday, Sunday and Monday, when Monday is a holiday.

***Tomb of the Unknown [Soldier]** *(noun)* – the burial room or grave in Arlington National Cemetery that is a monument that honors all unknown soldiers who died in battle.

veteran *(noun)* – any person leaving the military service with a record of good behavior.

***Veterans Administration** *(noun)* – a part of the government responsible for the care of veterans.

—— Thanksgiving Day ——

Thanksgiving is a holiday to thank God for his <u>blessings</u>. It is the oldest American holiday and has a very long tradition behind it. It started as a religious holiday, but it has become less religious in modern times. Many Americans know little about the beginning of Thanksgiving.

The Pilgrims

The story of Thanksgiving begins with the Pilgrims. They were a group of Christians who lived in England in the 1500's. The word *pilgrim* means "foreigner, alien or wanderer." They wanted to worship God freely and follow teachings from the Bible. They believed their lives on earth were a journey until they died and went to heaven. Worshipping God was an important part of their journey.

A new law in England in 1534 made the king the new religious leader in that country. This law required everyone to be a member of the new Church of England, even if they didn't want to be a church member. Many English people did not agree with this law.

The Pilgrims did not agree about how they should respond to this law. Some wanted to stay in the Church of England and make it better. They were called <u>Puritans</u>. This word means "purify or clean." Others wanted to leave the church, so they were called "<u>Separatists</u>." The Separatists continued to call themselves "Pilgrims," and that is what they are still called today. Puritans and Pilgrims both believed in God and the Bible. There were fewer than 1,000 Pilgrims and many more Puritans.

Thanksgiving

4th Thursday
in November

Pilgrims stopped going to worship services in churches. Instead they had Bible studies in their homes. The king said these meetings at home were against the law. English soldiers put Pilgrims in jail and treated them badly. Many of them were afraid and wanted to leave England. In 1607 many went to Leyden (pronounced LIE den), a small city in Holland. Then in 1618 King James I said that all Pilgrims in England must either obey the church or leave the country. Most of them quickly left.

Leyden, Holland

The Pilgrims were honest, hardworking people. In Leyden they already had the freedom to worship as they chose. But they had two big problems. First, they were poor internationals who made very little money. Second, they wanted to worship in their native language, English. Their children were forgetting English and learning to speak Dutch, the language in Holland. These problems caused them to think that God wanted them to sail to America to start a new life. Then they could speak English and worship God freely in a new land. They borrowed money from a trading company and prepared two ships that would take them to America – the *Speedwell*, and the now famous *Mayflower*.

The Pilgrims got on the *Speedwell* and began sailing on July 22, 1620 for the city of Southampton to join those on the *Mayflower*. This ship had almost 80 people on it. Most of these "strangers" did not care about the Pilgrims. They were going to America to find riches in North America. Both ships sailed together on August 5th, but water leaked into the *Speedwell*. This forced them to go back to Plymouth. After they found more leaks, they sold the *Speedwell* and <u>squeezed</u> as many people and supplies as possible into the *Mayflower*. Finally, 102 men, women and children began sailing again.

Sailing Across the Atlantic

In the middle of the Atlantic, a very bad storm almost sank the ship, but they kept going. On November 9th, someone saw land and cried, "Land, ho!" They discovered that the storm blew them north to Cape Cod, part of Massachusetts. This was over 100 miles north of Virginia where they had planned to go. If they stayed in Cape Cod, they would be free from the New England Company because it controlled business in Virginia, but not in Massachusetts. They decided the storm was God's way of directing them to a new place. So they stayed in Massachusetts and wrote the *Mayflower Compact*, a plan for their government. The Pilgrims wrote four reasons why they came to America. Each reason is followed by the words they wrote in the Compact.

Thanksgiving

4th Thursday
in November

1. To take Christianity to new areas:
   "Having [begun], for the glory of God, and
   advancement of the Christian Faith . . ."

2. To build a new home in the New World:
   ". . . to plant the first <u>colony</u> in the northern parts . . ."

3. To make a united form of government:
   "combine ourselves together into a civil body politic"

4. To make only the laws that are good for everyone:
   " . . . make such just and equal laws . . . .
   for the general good."

Plymouth

The Pilgrims found land for farming that was already cleared of rocks and trees. Four freshwater creeks provided water nearby. They named their <u>colony</u> *Plymouth* because they received help from Christians back in Plymouth, England. They lived in the *Mayflower* until they built their homes. On January 14th, a fire on the roof of the Common House (where they held meetings) almost killed everyone. From December, 1620 through March, 1621 forty-seven died of disease, including 13 of the 18 wives. Even though almost half of them died, those still living were grateful to be alive.

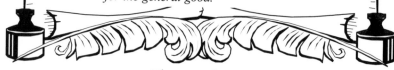

Thanksgiving

4th Thursday
in November

Getting to Know the Natives

In the middle of March, 1621 a <u>Native American</u> walked into the Common House. The Pilgrims were having a class about protecting themselves. "Welcome!" he said in perfect English. He then asked them for something to eat. They gave him only English food they brought from England and he enjoyed it all. After eating, he told them his name was Samoset. He was from a northern <u>tribe</u> and loved to travel. He learned English from traveling with English sea captains. He told them that the land the Pilgrims settled on belonged to the Patuxet Indians. An unknown illness had killed all the Patuxets four years before the Pilgrims arrived.

Samoset returned one week later with another native who also spoke English. His name was Squanto. He was *a Patuxet!* Squanto's story is interesting. In 1605 Englishmen caught him and four other Patuxets and took them back to England. They learned to speak English there. Then he returned to his homeland 9 years later. A short time later another English sea captain forced him to go back to Spain and sold him as a slave. Some Christians bought him and taught him about the Christian faith. Then they set him free. Squanto slowly got back to England. He finally returned to America in 1619, one year before the Pilgrims traveled to America. Six months before the Pilgrims landed, he learned that his entire tribe was dead. Therefore, he lived with another native tribe.

Massasoit, the most important native leader in that area, came to meet the Pilgrims. Samoset was an <u>interpreter</u> so they could talk to each other. The two groups agreed not to fight each other for forty years. They promised to help each other in many ways. They celebrated their friendship by making speeches and giving gifts.

A Feast

Later the Pilgrims chose a day for public thanksgiving to God to be held in October. They invited Chief Massasoit. He arrived one day early with 90 other natives! But they brought with them 5 deer, more than 12 fat, wild turkeys (all killed and ready to cook), and eight different types of vegetables. The Indian women taught the Pilgrim wives how to make many native foods like fruit pies, maple <u>syrup</u> and popcorn! When they were not eating, they played different games and sporting contests. The celebration went so well, they continued the feast for 3 more days!

Date of the Holiday

Thanksgiving Day

4th Thursday in November

Over the years Thanksgiving celebrations spread throughout areas of the United States. America's first president, George Washington, said in 1789,

I . . . [make] Thursday, the 26th day of November next to be devoted by the people of these States to the service of that great and glorious [God], Who is the . . . Author of all the good that was, that is, or that will be; that we may then all unite in . . . humble thanks for His kind care and protection of the people of this country . . .

47

In 1863 President Abraham Lincoln said the national holiday should be on the last Thursday in November. Finally in 1941, when Franklin D. Roosevelt was president, Thanksgiving was declared to be on the fourth Thursday of November.

Modern Celebrations

Much of the food cooked for modern Thanksgiving dinners includes items from the very first celebration – turkey, ham, <u>dressing</u>, potatoes with gravy, and many other vegetables, bread and pies for dessert. The first meal was held to thank God for protection and providing enough food for the winter.

Many families put a <u>horn of plenty</u> on their dining tables. It is also called a *cornucopia,* which means "abundance." The very first cornucopia was a curved goat's horn laid on the table filled with fruit and grain. Modern cornucopias are often made of plastic or straw like a basket and filled with fruit or vegetables.

<u>Parades</u> also are a part of American Thanksgiving celebration. They began in the late 1800's. Modern "<u>Turkey Day</u>" parades include a number of popular media stars, marching bands, <u>floats</u>, large <u>helium</u> balloons. Floats and balloon figures provide family entertainment for the crowds and TV viewers. Santa Claus sits on the last float of the Thanksgiving parade. He is the favorite, nonreligious symbol of Christmas and gifts [see Christmas]. When Santa arrives, the Christmas shopping season officially begins. The day after Thanksgiving is the busiest shopping day of the year.

Thanksgiving

4th Thursday in November

Most modern Thanksgiving celebrating is centered on the family. This began in the 1800's. <u>Relatives</u> often travel great distances to celebrate together. Thanksgiving weekend is the busiest travel time of the whole year in the US.

Many American churches have special Thanksgiving services when people remember God's goodness, especially family and friends. As television became popular, football became a regular part of Thanksgiving for many families. But the sporting events at the first Thanksgiving and football games on TV today are not related. Thanksgiving remains a special holiday when people enjoy God's blessings.

Vocabulary

blessings *(noun)* – an act of making something holy.

colony *(noun)* – a group of people who have moved to another area, but are still governed by their home country.

dressing *(noun)* – stuffing cooked with chicken, fish, etc.

float *(noun)* – a colorful display set on wheels in a parade.

*helium *(noun)* – a gas, like air but lighter than air, that makes things like balloons float upwards.

*horn of plenty *(noun)* – during harvest season, a table decoration in the shape of a horn that usually has fruit or vegetables inside.

interpreter *(noun)* – a person who expresses the meaning of words in one language in another language.

*Native American *(noun)* – American Indian.

parade *(noun)* – an orderly movement of people in colorful or formal dress or uniforms, usually to show pride or to honor a special day or event.

*Puritans *(noun)* – people living in 16th Century England who wanted to purify, or correct, the Church of England instead of leaving the church.

relatives *(noun)* – persons connected by blood or marriage to someone.

*Separatist *(noun)* – a person living in 16th Century England who thought the Church of England could not be corrected, and wanted to separate, or leave, the church.

squeeze *(verb)* – to press from two or more sides.

syrup *(noun)* – a thick, sweet liquid made from sugar cane, maple sugar, or other natural sugars.

tribe *(noun)* – a group of people with common customs and ancestry.

*Turkey Day *(noun)* – an informal name for Thanksgiving.

Christmas

Christmas is the celebration of the birth of Jesus Christ. His coming to earth is one of the most important events of history. Most calendars for the last 2,000 years have been based on his birth. Christmas became a national holiday in the US in 1890. Although it is a religious holiday, many modern Christmas customs and practices have come from other religious and nonreligious festivals. What follows is the history of the American Christmas celebration.

The birth and life of Jesus can be found in the Bible, in the New Testament books of Matthew (chapters 1-2) and Luke (chapter 2). These two books, along with Mark and John, are called *gospels,* meaning "stories of good news." God promised hundreds of years before that Jesus would be born in the town of Bethlehem in Israel. He would be God's <u>unique</u>, personal messenger. Jesus came to earth to bring peace with God. His birth, which was announced by angels who filled a night sky (see Luke 2:9-14), was good news. <u>Shepherds</u> were the first visitors to see the newborn Baby. Later wisemen, called *Magi,* traveled "from the east," to worship the Child and give him gifts (see Matthew 2:1-12). Christians in the first two hundred years after Jesus' birth did not celebrate his birth. They thought celebrating birthdays was a pagan (non-Christian) custom. However, the holiday developed slowly, beginning around 200 AD.

Christmas

December 25th

Date

The exact date of Christ's birth is not known. The December 25th date was a result of an attempt to <u>Christianize</u> a pagan festival known as *Saturnalia,* which began December 17th. This holiday was known for its <u>continual</u> parties. In 274 AD Roman Emperor Aurelian said that December 25th would be the holiday of the Syrian sun god for the whole empire. December 25th is the time when the sun is farthest away from the northern part of the earth; it is also the time when longer daylight begins. But in 336 AD the Roman Emperor Constantine said that December 25th would be the day to celebrate Christ's birth, trying to include Christians in celebrations. When the empire divided into two parts, east and west, the church in the east (Eastern Orthodox) changed their Christmas date to January 6th. Many countries still use January 6th as the birth date of Christ. The time between December 25th and January 6th is called the "12 Days of Christmas."

Names

The word *Christmas* comes from the early English phrase, *Christes Masse,* meaning "Christ's mass." *Mass* is the name of the Roman Catholic Church's worship service. Another name for this season is *Advent,* meaning "coming" or "arrival." This speaks of the coming of the *Messiah,* a Hebrew word meaning "chosen one." The idea is that God chose a special person to send to earth to bring peace. The Greek word *Christ* means the same thing as *Messiah.* The name *Yule* comes from <u>Scandinavia</u>. The Yule was a large log that started the fire in the fireplace in honor of the god, Thor. When people in Scandinavia became Christians, "Yuletide" became Christmas time. Another word, *noel,* means "carol," or song. The abbreviation "Xmas" comes from the Greek letter, *chi* (X), which begins Christ's name in the Greek language.

Saint Nicholas / Santa Claus

Saint Nicholas was a real person who lived in the 4th Century in ancient Asia Minor (modern day Turkey). He was a rich man and a Christian pastor. He used his money to help <u>sailors,</u> poor and homeless people, and children, especially <u>orphans</u>. He gave away so much money that he became famous all over the world. On Christmas he secretly delivered gifts to children in <u>orphanages.</u> Many Greek and Russian churches made him the <u>saint</u> of gifts, sailors, scholars, unmarried women and children.

Christmas

December 25th

The modern American Santa Claus is not the same person as the older Saint Nicholas, but they both use the same name. Early Dutch settlers in New York called Saint Nicholas *Sinterklaas,* which became "Santa Claus." Over the years the American Santa became <u>similar</u> to the British Santa, known as "Father Christmas." Both would enter a house through the <u>chimney</u>

and fill long socks, called "stockings," hung near the chimney. This idea came from an old Scandinavian story.

The American Santa became better defined in the 1800's. Clement Moore in 1822 first wrote that Santa wore a red suit with white fur and drove a <u>sled</u> pulled by reindeer in his poem, "Twas the Night Before Christmas." Later <u>cartoonist</u> Thomas Nast drew several pictures that showed Santa as a fat, friendly, winter visitor dressed in red clothing. St. Nicholas in both England and America leaves toys and other gifts for children on Christmas Eve, the night of December 24th. The American Santa Claus is the center of the cultural, nonreligious part of Christmas. He had no part of the beginning of the holiday.

Christmas Tree / House Decorations

The Christmas tree came from the "miracle plays" held in Germany from 900-1400 AD. Actors performed on flat wagons pulled by horses that moved from town to town. These wagons looked like a stage on wheels. The plays were about the miracles of Jesus and early Christians. One play was about the creation of the world. The only thing on the stage was the "Paradise Tree" — a <u>fir tree</u> with apples on it. Since this play ended with the promise of Christ's coming, <u>dramas</u> were performed during the Advent (Christmas) season. By the 1500's people began using fir trees for their personal Christmas celebrations. Tradition says that Martin Luther, the priest who began the Reformation [see Halloween], was the

Christmas

December 25th

first to put candles on a Christmas tree. German immigrants brought the tree custom to America in 1710. Electric lights were first put on a Christmas tree in 1895 by Ralph Morris who worked for the telephone company. Ornaments on today's trees are different from country to country.

Many people enjoy putting plants in and around their homes. Scandinavians think <u>mistletoe</u> brings peace and good will. Others like to hang up fir tree branches, <u>wreaths</u> and <u>holly</u>. Since Christmas colors are red and green, people use poinsettias, a green plant with red flowers from Mexico. Today most American poinsettias come from California, and most of the world's mistletoe is grown in Central Texas.

Christmas Cards / Gift Giving

The custom of sending Christmas cards began about 150 years ago. People first sent holiday notes written by hand. Then artist John Calcott Horsley made the first Christmas card in 1843. By the late 1860's, Christmas cards were as common as handwritten notes. Around 1875 the first colored cards appeared. Today about three billion Christmas cards are sent each year.

The giving of gifts has two possible beginnings. First, Christians point to the wisemen who gave gifts of gold, <u>frankincense</u> and <u>myrrh</u> to the Baby Jesus. Second, the custom could have come from Saint Nicholas's tradition of giving gifts. Both are pictures of the kindness and love that God showed when he gave his Son to the world. Christians and non-Christians enjoy the custom of showing love for others by giving gifts.

Christmas Carols

The first Christmas songs were written in the 400's AD and were similar to other church songs, called *hymns*. They were written in Latin, the common language of the church at that time. Most of them are about religious themes. Carols *(noels)* were first written around 1000 AD. They are simple songs about the Gospel (the story of Jesus) with more human and personal interests. Their music style sounds happier than hymns.

As people in Europe added dramas and plays to Christmas celebrations, carols became an important part. When the plays were done, singers, called *carolers,* walked home singing in the streets. This is how street caroling began. Many of the traditional favorite Christmas carols, such as "O Come, All Ye Faithful" and "Silent Night," were written in the 1800's. Christmas songs such as "Jingle Bells" and "White Christmas" came later and show the cultural part of the holiday. Handel's famous *Messiah* is an oratorio − a musical drama with no stage background. It was first performed in 1742 and quickly became a Christmas favorite. Music <u>experts</u> agree that Christmas music is part of the best music ever written.

Christmas

December 25th

Star / Lights

People use lights and stars as ornaments in Christmas decorations. Some believe this idea came from *Saturnalia*, the holiday celebrating longer daylight. Others think this custom began with the Star of Bethlehem when Jesus was born (Matthew 2:1-2). Thus, people put stars on the top of Christmas trees or roofs. Christians point to the Bible and say that Christmas lights around their homes represent Jesus who said, "I am the light of the world" (John 8:12).

Nativity Scenes

Many Americans set up a small <u>nativity scene</u> in their homes, often under their Christmas trees. Some families set up larger ones outside in their yard. These contain an image of Baby Jesus in his first bed, which is called a *manger*. A manger is a feeding box for animals. In the scene with Jesus are his mother, Mary, and her husband Joseph. With them are shepherds, wisemen, a few angels and some farm animals. This custom began on Christmas Eve, 1223AD by Saint Francis of Assisi in a cave near the town of Greccio, Italy. Saint Francis was a famous Christian and wanted to re-create the scene of Jesus' birth.

Foods

Like Christmas <u>ornaments</u>, foods served for Christmas dinner are different from family to family and from country to country. A Christmas dinner in an American family's home includes turkey (or sometimes chicken, duck, goose or ham) and <u>dressing</u>, potatoes and gravy, sweet potatoes, green vegetables, cranberry sauce, nuts, fruits, fruit cake, pumpkin and other pies, and sweets. <u>Eggnog</u> is usually the favorite drink for the whole family.

Candy Canes

Christmas

December 25th

The red and white striped candy cane is a favorite candy of Christmas time. Tradition says a candy maker in Indiana created it. He used many of the ideas of Christmas in his plan for the candy cane. The pure white represents the <u>innocence</u> of Jesus' life on earth. Most candy canes have red stripes on them. These stripes are like the ones made on Jesus' body when soldiers beat him with a whip before he died. The candy maker made the cane from hard candy. The hardness represents Jesus as "the Rock," another way to describe him. He made the top of the cane <u>curved</u> to look like a shepherd's staff because Jesus called himself "the Good Shepherd." If the cane is held upside down, it makes the letter 'J,' the first letter of the name Jesus.

Celebrations

Family Christmas customs are very different. Most families normally open gifts either on Christmas Eve or Christmas Day. Members may open them all at once, one at a time, or have some other type of family tradition. Some families will have a birthday cake for Jesus, and sing "Happy Birthday" to him. Other families sing Christmas carols together, share special Christmas stories, or do a family project that helps poor people.

Some people find this time of year depressing. It is caused by a number of reasons — from having no family around to celebrate with, to feeling poor or left out, etc. More people kill themselves during the Christmas season than at any other time of the year.

Christmas is about giving. Americans usually think of buying new gifts when they give to others. Thus they spend a lot of money during the Christmas season. That is why more money is spent at Christmas than at any other time of the year. Stores have special sales and are very crowded. Parking lots are full of cars. Christmas has become too <u>materialistic</u> for many people.

The idea of giving acts of service has become popular. Many churches help their city celebrate with special events such as Christmas <u>pageants</u> or concerts. They may help feed poor and homeless people, send gifts to prisoners and their families, or write letters to soldiers in the military. Most churches have special meetings (such as Christmas Eve services) or regular services with Christmas themes. All these activities are done at this time because God gave his son Jesus to the world. For Christians the Christmas spirit is giving to others and saying "Thank you" to God for sending Jesus.

Vocabulary

cartoonist *(noun)* – a person who draws a
   picture or pictures to make people laugh.

chimney *(noun)* – a large pipe or hollow brick
   structure that allows smoke from a fire
   or furnace to pass into the open air.

*Christianize *(verb)* – to make something more Christian in its
   nature or purpose.

Christmas

December 25th

continual *(adjective)* – happening without stopping.

curved *(adjective)* – something that is bent without angles.

drama *(noun)* – a play, especially a serious one, for acting on a stage.

dressing *(noun)* – stuffing cooked with chicken, fish, etc.

***eggnog** *(noun)* – a thick drink made of milk, eggs and spices usually drunk at Christmas time.

expert *(noun)* – a master at something.

fir tree *(noun)* – a type of tall pine tree with pointed leaves found in cool climates.

***frankincense** *(noun)* – a thick fluid from East African and Arabic trees that is used for perfume.

***holly** *(noun)* – green plant or tree that has thick shiny leaves and red berries.

innocence *(noun)* – a lack of guilt.

***materialistic** *(adjective)* – making material or physical things more important.

***mistletoe** *(noun)* – green plant that has thick leaves, small yellow flowers and white berries.

***myrrh** *(noun)* – a thick fluid from East African or Arabian trees used as a spice, perfume or healing cream.

***nativity scene** *(noun)* – a set of objects or figures that show the birth of Jesus in natural setting.

ornaments *(noun)* – a beautiful decoration; beautiful objects put on a Christmas tree.

orphan *(noun)* – a child whose parents have died.

***orphanage** *(noun)* – an institution or place where orphans live.

pageant *(noun)* – a colorful public entertainment, usually showing a famous historical event.

sailor *(noun)* – a person who works on a ship.

saint *(noun)* – a person chosen by God.

***Scandinavia** *(noun)* – the northern part of Europe.

***shepherd** *(noun)* – a person who takes care of sheep.

***similar** *(adjective)* – almost alike.

sled *(noun)* – a vehicle that slides down on runners over the snow.

unique *(adjective)* – singular, one of a kind.

wreaths *(noun)* – round or circular arrangements of flowers or leaves used for decoration.

New Year's Day

New Year's Day is a holiday celebrated everywhere in the world, but not on the same day! Celebrating New Year's on different days began with ancient cultures that had different <u>calendars</u>. Religions and cultural traditions made them different. For example, the ancient Egyptians celebrated New Year's in the middle of June, when the Nile River flooded the lowlands. Different reasons caused Chinese, Jewish, Roman and Islamic calendars to have different dates for their year's first day [see April Fool's Day].

In spite of the reasons, however, people celebrate every New Year in special ways with great happiness. Giving gifts is a major part of New Year celebrations in many countries. This custom started thousands of years ago when people brought gifts to religious temples. Janus was the old Roman god of gates and doors, as well as beginnings and endings. His picture shows him with two faces – one looking forward, the other looking backward. The word *January* comes from his name. People gave gifts to Janus because they thought, "My New Year will be better if I bring a gift to Janus." They also gave gifts to many important government leaders on New Year's Day.

Visiting friends and family members has been part of New Year celebrations in some countries. Since people did not travel very much in the past, New Year's gave people a reason to visit others they normally did not see during the year. They would talk about what happened the year before and ask about plans for the future.

Long ago people in England believed that cleaning their <u>chimneys</u> would bring them good luck. So cleaning a chimney on New Year's Day would bring good luck the whole year! This custom was practiced there for hundreds of years. It also created the saying, *Clean the slate,* which means, "wipe the dust off this flat surface." Today this phrase means "forget what is past and begin again or start over."

New Year's Day in the US has five main customs. The first is New Year's Eve parties, when people celebrate the hopes and dreams for the coming year. The national symbol of this is the great ball on top of a building in Times Square in New York City. The ball has the number of the New Year on it and moves down on a pole very slowly. The number of the year cannot be seen until the New Year comes. Over a million people gather there to count down the last hours and minutes of the old year. They sing, shout, dance and kiss! Many people raise their drinks to <u>toast</u> the New Year. The passing of the old year seems to make Americans more hopeful for the new year. Most Americans cannot explain this hope they have.

The second New Year custom is celebrating with <u>fireworks</u> on New Year's Eve. In most parts of the US people need permission from the government to use fireworks. Many people will stay up very late. Then at midnight they light firecrackers, rockets and <u>flares</u> to celebrate the New Year. This custom is like the Chinese custom of fireworks at New Year's.

The third tradition is the number of football "<u>bowl</u>" <u>games</u> that appear on television. The last week of the year has at least one football game each night on TV that can be seen anywhere in the country. This custom is not really a custom created by the New Year. Many games are played because the football season ends near the end of the year. But some people believe football and New Year's are related in some way.

New Year's Day

January 1st

The fourth custom of New Year's is the parade. Similar to Thanksgiving Day parades [see Thanksgiving], many <u>floats</u>, marching bands, huge balloons in many shapes are important parts of these parades. They happen in the morning and can be seen on television. They represent the happiness and celebration of the first day of the New Year.

The fifth custom is New Year's resolutions. A resolution is a decision to improve personal behavior by making changes. Examples of resolutions are: stop smoking, stop drinking, start on a diet, begin saving (more) money, read a number of books each year, or almost any other change that makes them better. Not all people make resolutions, but many do. By the end of January most people who made a resolution quit or stop the change. This is called, "breaking the resolution." This happens because new <u>habits</u> are hard to start and old habits are hard to stop. Resolutions show that Americans know they need to make changes, but many do not have a good plan to help them make those changes.

Many churches in America will have a special meeting on New Year's Eve called a "<u>Watch Night" Service</u>. During this service Christians will pray, enjoy friendship with each other, share personal <u>testimonies</u>, light candles and listen to Bible teaching. Like the two-faced Janus, Christians look back at the old year. They remember God's goodness to them the past year. They also look forward to the New Year by thinking about things God wants them to do. Some Christians make decisions or commitments to obey God more during the New Year. They are like resolutions. Whether resolutions are religious or not, the New Year is a good time to start again.

Vocabulary

*bowl games *(noun)* – important football games played in stadiums that look like huge bowls and have different names.

calendar *(noun)* – a chart of the days and months of a year or years.

chimney *(noun)* – the large metal pipe or hollow brick structure for passing smoke from a fire or furnace into the open air.

fireworks *(noun)* – a show of light, colorful explosives for celebration.

*flare *(noun)* – a fire or light used to signal or attract attention.

float *(noun)* – a colorful display set on wheels in a parade.

habit *(noun)* – something you do often.

*testimonies *(noun)* – true stories about people's past religious experiences.

toast (verb) – to honor someone (or something), especially with a drink.

Watch Night Service *(noun)* – a special church meeting held on New Year's Eve that encourages people to be more obedient to God in the New Year.

Martin Luther King Day

Martin Luther King Day is the newest national holiday in the US. It is celebrated on January 15th, the birthday of <u>civil rights</u> leader, Martin Luther King. He did many important things in a short time.

Martin was born in 1929 in Atlanta, Georgia. He was the second child of <u>Pastor</u> Michael King and a very good student in school. After high school he attended Morehouse College and graduated with a Bachelor of Arts degree in 1948. He later attended Crozer Theological Seminary, a religious school, and then received a doctorate degree in 1955 from Boston University. During his time in Boston, he met Coretta Scott and married her in 1953. A year later he became pastor of the Dexter Avenue Baptist Church in Montgomery, Alabama.

Martin
Luther
King Day

January 15th

Slavery had been a custom in the South for over 200 years. Abraham Lincoln, America's 16th President [see President's Day], freed the Blacks from slavery in 1863, in the middle of the Civil War. But Blacks and Whites did things differently. Many times they did not understand each other. State laws required segregation, a policy that kept Blacks and Whites separated. In restaurants Whites ate in one room; Blacks ate in another. On public buses Blacks sat in the back; Whites sat in the front. Even simple things like restrooms and water fountains were separate. In some places Blacks were not permitted to eat in some restaurants, shop in certain stores, visit a few parks or go to some schools. This separation happened all over the southern part of the US. Blacks had little hope that it would ever change.

One day a lady named Rosa Parks decided to do something about it. Rosa did not give up her seat to a white man on a full bus. Her action started a national debate about the differences between groups of people and how they should act toward each other. Martin Luther King helped organize a one-year boycott of the bus company that made Blacks give up their seats to Whites. Newspapers reported his work across the country and he became famous by 1956. Two years later he wrote his first book, *Stride Toward Freedom,* which explained his ideas. In 1960 he became a pastor with his father of Ebenezer Baptist Church in Atlanta. Later that year the Southern Christian Leadership Conference (SCLC), a civil rights group, chose him to be their leader.

Dr. King believed that things would get better. He wanted to change the laws white Americans made about Blacks. His "I Have A Dream" speech in Washington, DC, in 1964 was truly his finest hour. *Time* magazine named him "Man of the Year." Later that same year he received the Nobel (Peace) Prize, the first black American to win it. At age 35, he was also the youngest person ever to win this award.

By 1965 King saw that segregation was keeping Blacks poor and hurt their chance to make more money. Therefore he called for a "revolution of values," and asked the government for economic help for Blacks. More people joined him and helped in his marches, boycotts and rallies. Some people thought these new workers were not really interested in helping Blacks, but wanted to help themselves. By 1968 he returned to Washington, DC, demanding a $12 billion "Economic Bill of Rights" for black Americans. By this time some Americans stopped supporting him. They did not agree with this demand for economic help from the government and thought it was not a good idea.

In April 1968, in the middle of this work in Washington, King went to Memphis, Tennessee. He wanted to help support a strike by workers who pick up garbage. While he stood on an open patio of the second floor in the back of the motel where he was staying, a gunman, James Earl Ray, shot King on April 4th. King died that night at the age of 39. King read, believed in and taught the teachings of Jesus. He also followed the example of peacefully protesting things in society taught by India's former leader, Mohandas Gandhi. King did not die peacefully. In the next few months, many

Martin Luther King Day

January 15th

61

people who were angry about King's death caused a lot of trouble in cities around the US. <u>Riots</u>, fires, shooting, stealing, and fighting happened everyday for weeks. It took a long time for the police and the military to stop the riots. Ray finally said he shot King and went to prison. Later he changed his story, but he died there in 1998.

More than any other man in America, Martin Luther King made Americans aware of the struggles of a <u>minority</u> group (Blacks) in the country. He taught how people were similar in many ways. He also said our differences should not separate us; we should understand and accept each other. History sees him to be one of the most important leaders of <u>diversity</u>, a belief that understanding the differences in human beings is good. In 1983 the Congress of the United States passed a law that made King's birthday, January 15th, a national holiday. Because some Americans did not agree with his ideas, it took years before all the states obeyed the new holiday law. Celebrations include rallies, speeches, marches, and movies or special programs on television about King's life and the history of civil rights. King is important in American history. Some of his statements are famous around the world.

The values of brotherhood, love and understanding others are ideas King taught. He learned them from the Bible. It says that God does not treat people differently because of how they look. God tells his people to do the same. Martin Luther King's gift to us is that the well being of all people of any race, language, cultural or national background, should be important to everyone.

Martin Luther King Day

January 15th

Vocabulary

boycott *(noun)* – the action of deciding for political reasons not to buy products or do business with a company.

civil rights *(noun)* – in the USA, the rights of each citizen guaranteed by the Constitution, such as the rights to vote and not suffer prejudice because of race, nationality, etc.

diversity *(noun)* – differences among people in race, ethnic group, religion, etc.

*march *(noun)* – a public demonstration of people walking together from one point to another to display a common opinion.

minority *(adjective)* – related to people of a different race, background or religion from those of the majority of people in a nation.

Nobel Prize *(noun)* – an award given each year in the following areas: physical sciences, medicine, economics, literature and efforts toward world peace.

pastor *(noun)* – a minister in charge of a church.

rallies *(noun)* – meetings of people to excite them about an idea, product or sports event.

revolution *(noun)* – a big change, sometimes caused by force or war, especially in a government economy, or field of study.

riot *(noun)* – an act of violent behavior by a large group.

strike *(noun)* – a work stoppage because of disagreements with management.

─── Valentine's Day ───

Valentine's Day is a one-day celebration of <u>romance</u> and love held on February 14th. It began in ancient Greek and Roman culture and later the church changed it. We will look at their traditions in historical order.

The Romans had many gods they worshipped. *Lupercalia* was a festival that celebrated a god and goddess on February 15th. Faunus was an Italian god of the farmland who later was compared to Pan, the god of nature and herds. Ceremonies were held at Lupercal, a cave in the Palatine Hill. People believed this cave was also the home of Juno, the goddess of women and marriage. Celebrations included each woman choosing a man to show signs of love and give gifts to. These relationships continued long alter the festival ended, and many couples got married.

Because of the love shown in *Lupercalia* festival, people began to include Cupid, the Roman god of love. His Greek name was Eros. The first pictures of Cupid show him to be a strong, good looking young man with wings. By the mid-300's BC, he had changed to a fat baby with wings who carried a bow and arrows. People believed when Cupid shot an arrow at someone, that person would fall in love. (The arrow did not hurt.) Cupid and hearts are still the main <u>symbols</u> in modern Valentine's Day cards and gifts.

Especially for...
Valentine's Day

February 14th

At that time Christianity was a new religion. At first many people did not believe in it. There were few Christians and others did not welcome them. Some were beaten, thrown in jail, and lost their jobs or homes. It was not proper to help Christians. Valentine was a Christian pastor who lived in Rome when Claudius II was emperor in the 200's AD. He was put in jail for helping Christians. Tradition says while he was in jail he wrote of love to a female friend. Valentine was a man who was true to his faith. He loved and helped those around him. Even the fear of death did not stop him. Sometime around 270 AD soldiers took Valentine out of jail and killed him on the Palatine Hill, the place of Juno's celebrations. He was buried in the St. Praxedes Church in Rome.

When Europeans started believing in Christianity, the Roman Catholic Church tried to give Christian meaning to holidays [see Halloween]. Valentine's life and work was a real example of Christian love. Church leaders thought he was a good choice for a holiday to replace the *Lupercalia* festival. So in 496 AD, Pope Gelasius moved *Lupercalia* to February 14th, one day earlier and changed its name to Saint Valentine's Day. However, these changes did not remove the feelings and actions of love that were shown during *Lupercalia*.

European countries have many Valentine traditions and customs. The earliest customs go back to the 1400's. At that time, English poet Geoffrey Chaucer, author of *Canterbury Tales,* first saw birds in pairs on February 14th. Many customs still involve girls and boys becoming a couple for a day to be each other's "Valentine." They share Valentine gifts with each other. Single females tried magic tricks to help them "catch" a man that they might marry later. In England during the 1700's, love letters between Valentines replaced gifts as the main custom of the holiday.

Valentine celebrations in America began in the 1800's. By 1863 a magazine article said that Valentine's Day had become the most celebrated holiday in the world other than Christmas. Modern children celebrate Valentine's Day by making cards for friends and family members in school. These cards are red and white, include hearts and lace paper, and contain words of love and friendship. Pictures of Cupid, hearts and arrows can be seen on many cards in stores. These cards contain messages of love, care or sometimes humor. Over one billion cards are sent each year.

Adults celebrate the day with actions and gifts of love to their Valentine (their husband or wife, girlfriend or boyfriend). Things like flowers, candy, a romantic night out, a favorite meal, a special gift or almost anything else that is special is the custom for Valentine's. Ministers in churches may give talks on the love of God. Some couples even get married on

Valentine's Day. Whether we think of Cupid, marriage or God, Valentine's Day makes people remember that love is an important part of life and should be celebrated.

Vocabulary

couple *(noun)* – two people (usually a female and a male) who are married, living together, or in a relationship.

humor *(noun)* – something funny in written, spoken or printed form.

lace *(noun)* – material, such as silk, made by hand or machine into fine decorative patterns.

magazine *(noun)* – a small weekly, or monthly, publication that usually includes news, stories, and photos.

magic *(adjective)* – related to the use of forces outside the laws of nature to make something happen.

romance *(noun)* – a love affair with excitement, adventure and happiness.

romantic *(adjective)* – related to love or romance.

symbol *(noun)* – a sign, mark, picture, object, or event that represents something else.

— Presidents' Day —

Presidents' Day was created by combining the birthdays of two American presidents: George Washington and Abraham Lincoln. It began when Americans first celebrated Washington's birthday, February 22nd. Later Lincoln's birthday, February 12th, was added because of his accomplishments. Since both birthdays are in February, leaders in the government chose to honor both men on the third Monday in February. This day always comes between the two presidents' birthdays.

Washington is called "The Father of his country" and is famous around the world. He was born in 1732 in Pope's Creek, VA, the oldest son of Augustine and Mary Washington. His father died when George was only 11. He wanted to join the British Navy but his mother would not let him. Then he worked for a man who measured land. The knowledge he gained would be helpful later in battle. In 1753 he helped the British army as a <u>scout</u> in the French and Indian War. After a successful time in the military, he entered politics in 1759. People chose him to be a leader in Virginia. Earlier that year he married Martha Custis, a rich widow who had two children, John and "Patsy." They had no children of their own.

Presidents' Day

3rd Monday in February

At that time Great Britain had many <u>colonies</u> all over the world. But the American colonies were larger and different from the other British colonies. The number of people moving to America was growing quickly. Cities were becoming large, and trade with Britain was increasing. However, disagreements between the American colonies and Great Britain had also been growing for some time. Britain found it more and more difficult to control the American colonies.

By 1769, Washington was leading Virginia in its disagreements against England. After two meetings in 1774-1775, a group of American colony leaders, called the Continental Congress [see Independence Day], chose him to be the leader of the colonial military on July 3, 1775. Washington lost more battles than he won, but his army surrounded and captured the British soldiers at Yorktown, VA on September 28, 1781. The Americans had won the war and their freedom! During the war soldiers told stories of Washington's concern for them and his faith in God. Some soldiers saw him on his knees, alone in the woods, praying for his soldiers' safety and success in the war. This made him more famous. Most people loved him.

After the war Washington wanted to return to his beautiful home, Mount Vernon. It was a large piece of land with five farms. He grew many crops there, including wheat and fruit trees. Washington was an excellent farmer, but his countrymen had other ideas for the general.

In 1787 they chose him to be Virginia's leader for the meeting that would make a new government. This meeting was called the Constitutional Convention [see Independence Day] because they created the government by writing the US Constitution. Then the people voted for Washington to become the first President of the United States. He began his first four-year <u>term</u> as president on April 30, 1789. It was a peaceful four years. The people chose him again to another term in 1792. His second term was more difficult. Some people disagreed with a few of his ideas. He decided not to serve a third term. His last speech in 1797, called a "Farewell Address," be-

came an important part of America's policy toward other countries for over a hundred years. After being home again for less than three years, Washington became sick. Doctors could not save him, and he died December 14, 1799.

People everywhere loved Washington for his honesty, his faith in God, and his care for others. One friend described him as being "First in war, first in peace, and first in the hearts of his countrymen." People all across the country were very sad for months after he died. They wanted to make his birthday a national holiday. Washington, DC and the <u>Washington Monument</u> are named for him. He appears on the one dollar bill and 25 cent quarter.

No one thought Abraham Lincoln would become a great person. Called "Honest Abe," he was born in 1809 in Kentucky within ten years of Washington's death. His father Thomas never studied in a school, but he was a very good carpenter. Abraham's mother Nancy died when he was only 9 years old. This made him very sad. The next year his father married Sarah Bush Johnston. Abraham liked her, and she continued to teach him the Bible. Abraham loved to read any book he could get. Many nights he read by candlelight, the only light in his family's dark log cabin.

Kentucky was a state where families could own slaves. Because his family's church taught against slavery, they would not own slaves. They moved to Indiana, a state where slavery was against the law. States in the north, like Indiana, were called "free" states, because everyone was free and no one was a slave. Southern states were called "slave" states [see Martin Luther King Day].

In 1828 he took his first trip, traveling down the Mississippi River to New Orleans. Two years later he moved to Illinois, and in 1831 settled near Springfield. The next year he tried to be elected for the state government, but not enough people voted for him. He won the next election in 1834 and worked in the government until 1841. During that time he became a lawyer and married Mary Todd on November 4, 1842. They had four sons.

In 1847 he served one 4-year term in the US House of Representatives. In 1856 he joined the new Republican Party because it was strongly against slavery. He debated Stephen Douglas seven times for the US Senate election in 1858. Lincoln's beliefs, clear thinking and powerful speaking showed many people around the country that he had great leadership skills. Lincoln won the debates but lost the election.

Presidents' Day

3rd Monday in February

The Republican Party chose Lincoln for the 1860 election for President. They believed Lincoln understood the problems of slavery better than anyone. In the election he received the most votes among several men. Democrats divided their votes between two men — one from the north against slavery and one from the south who was for slavery. This division helped Lincoln win. He became the nation's sixteenth president. People in the south believed Lincoln and the "antislavery" Republicans' victory ended any hopes of keeping slavery there. When he began his term in March 1861, the Southern states already had separated themselves from the <u>Union</u>. Five weeks later the Civil War began. It would be the worst time in American history. More men would die in this war – about 500,000 – than any other US war. People in the North and South had angry feelings toward each other for years. War began in South Carolina on April 12, 1861. Eighteen months later, on September 24, 1862 Lincoln showed great courage when he freed the slaves. The war continued and was fought in many places around the country. One terrible battle was fought in Gettysburg, PA. At the cemetery Lincoln gave a famous speech called the "Gettysburg Address." In this very short speech he told people his ideas about the war and his goals for the country. It is considered one of the best political speeches ever written. Lincoln said the saddest time in his life was when he saw all the dead soldiers at Gettysburg. He told a pastor at that time that he became a Christian after he visited Gettysburg. He said he needed God's help to continue leading the country.

Lincoln had many generals to lead the northern army. He chose Ulysses S. Grant in 1864 to be his top general. The Southern generals were much better military leaders. However, the South did not have enough supplies for their army like the North had. Many victories by the North helped Lincoln win election as president again. He wanted to rebuild the country in his second term. Finally the Southern Commanding General, Robert E. Lee, surrendered on April 9, 1865. The war was over.

Presidents' Day

3rd Monday in February

Five days later Lincoln and his wife went to a theater in Washington, DC to watch a play, *Our American Cousin*. He wanted to rest and celebrate the end of the war. John Wilkes Booth, a famous actor at that time, was angry at Lincoln for freeing the slaves. He went to the theater and found Lincoln's military guard drunk and asleep. Booth stepped past him and went upstairs where the president sat. He shot Lincoln in the back of his head with a small handgun. It was <u>Good Friday</u>, the weekend of the <u>Easter</u> celebration [see Easter]. People carried the president to the building across the street where doctors worked on him. Lincoln died the next morning at 7:22 AM. Booth was later caught and killed for shooting the president.

A train carried Lincoln's body from Washington across the country. Those who loved him called him "Father Abraham." He was buried in Springfield, IL on May 4th. Although the war was over, in many ways Lincoln became the last soldier to die. Abraham Lincoln was a special man during a difficult time. More than anything else, his clear thinking and faith in God kept the United States together. In his speech that began his second term as president, he said he wanted bad feelings "toward none" and "[love] for all." He lived his own life that way. Lincoln appears on the 5 dollar bill and the one cent penny. The Lincoln Memorial stands in the nation's capital to honor him.

Presidents' Day is a national holiday that honors Washington and Lincoln. Both of them are famous for their wisdom, strength and faith in God. Their actions show how much they believed God and the Bible, which they both read. They became examples of leadership for the rest of the country. This is why many people think these two men are the two greatest American presidents. Most celebrations of Presidents' Day will have historic themes. American flags, parades and speeches are common, as well as picnics and other activities.

Vocabulary

carpenter *(noun)* – a person who earns a living by making and building things with wood.

colony *(noun)* – a group of people who have moved to another area, but are still governed by their home country.

debated *(verb)* – argued, presented differing views on a question.

Easter *(noun)* – the Christian religious holiday celebrating Jesus Christ's return to life.

election *(noun)* – an event when people vote.

*Good Friday *(noun)* – the Friday before Easter when Jesus Christ died on a wooden cross.

Lincoln Memorial *(noun)* – a building in Washington, DC that honors Abraham Lincoln.

scout *(noun)* – a person sent out to collect information.

term *(noun)* – a time period, such as in elected office or education.

*union *(noun)* – the name used by Northerners to describe the United States.

Washington Monument *(noun)* – a building in Washington, DC that honors George Washington.

St. Patrick's Day

Saint Patrick's Day is March 17th of each year. It is a day to remember and honor the church leader of Ireland, Saint Patrick. March 17th is the day the Roman Catholic Church chose for the festival because it is the day tradition says he died. A brief history of him follows.

Patricius was born in 389 AD to a Christian family in southwestern Britain. This area was controlled by the Roman Empire. His parents taught him in the Christian faith, but he did not believe Christian teaching. When he was 16 years old, Irish slave hunters caught him and took him back to Ireland. They made him take care of pigs. While he was there he saw many Irish people who were not Christians. They followed another religion and were unkind to each other. This helped him understand that he needed God's forgiveness for his own sins. He decided to believe the Christian teaching his parents told him years before. He also knew that the Irish needed Christianity.

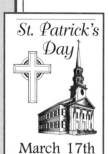

St. Patrick's Day

March 17th

Then one night after being a slave for six years, while he was praying, he thought of an idea how he could get free from the Irish. Patricius believed God gave him the plan. He followed the plan and gained his freedom. Then he took a ship to Gaul (modern day France) and later returned to his family in Britain.

For the next 20 years (412-431 AD) Patricius wanted to bring Christianity to Ireland. Therefore, he first returned to Gaul to study the Bible in the town of Auxerre with Saint Germanus. Germanus was a church leader in Auxerre and a missionary to Britain. When his studies were over, he went back to his family in Britain. They wanted Patricius to stop traveling, but were willing to help him serve God. Patricius believed God told him to go back to Ireland. Then he returned to

Auxerre where Germanus blessed him and sent him as Patrick, the Christian leader of the Irish, in 432 AD.

Patrick began his work in northern and western Ireland. Most of the Irish were not happy to see him. He wanted to visit his old owner, Miliucc, and share the Christian message with him. However, Miliucc heard that Patrick was coming to see him. He thought Patrick was angry at him, so Miliucc killed himself before Patrick arrived!

The poor of Ireland quickly believed Patrick's teaching. He knew that the rulers would need to believe his message before the whole country would change. However, the priests of the non-Christian religion called Druidism [see Halloween] controlled Irish society. Therefore, Patrick publicly debated them at Tara, the capital city of Ireland. Slowly he was able to help many leaders believe Christianity, including King Loegaire (pronounced LEER ee).

After many years of ministry, Patrick had trained 450 church leaders. They started over 300 new churches. Over 120,000 people became Christians. The country changed its laws to be more like biblical teachings. He also started religious communities and study centers called monasteries. Over the next several hundred years missionaries from these centers went all over Europe and were important in establishing Western culture. In spite of all these changes, the new Irish Christians disagreed with some ways of the Catholic Church. This did not make Catholic Church leaders in Europe happy. Some of them said Patrick should return to his home in England. He died in 461 AD.

Tradition says that Patrick would use a small 3-leaf plant, called a "clover" or a "shamrock," to represent the Trinity in his teaching. Thus finding a 4-leaf clover was very special and was a sign of God's blessing. Over the years this idea came to mean "good luck," and being "lucky." A common saying is "the luck of the Irish," and some people today still believe the Irish are lucky.

St. Patrick's Day

March 17th

Tradition also says that St. Patrick drove out the snakes from Ireland. This is more a legend than a real event. Some non-Christian religions often use the symbol of a snake. This was true of Druidism. When Ireland accepted Christianity, the snake symbol disappeared. This is probably where the idea came from.

Saint Patrick's Day is a festive event for people, but mainly for Catholics. On March 17th many people will drink green beer or wear green and gold colored clothing, the colors for the holiday. The green comes from green clovers. Later, a <u>childish</u> trick was added: If you didn't wear something green on that day, others would <u>pinch</u> you! Modern celebrations include parades, church services, picnics and parties. As with many holiday celebrations in America, it seems that most Americans know little about Saint Patrick's real life or the events that led to this holiday.

Vocabulary

blessing *(noun)* – an act of making something holy.

*childish *(adjective)* – relating to a child; immature.

luck *(noun)* – good fortune; success.

missionary *(noun)* – a person, especially a member of the clergy, who persuades others to accept his or her religion.

pinch *(verb)* – to press tightly between the thumb and a finger.

saint *(noun)* – a person chosen by God.

*sins *(noun)* – behaviors and actions that are against God's commands.

*Trinity *(noun)* – in Christian teaching, a word that describes the unity of the biblical God in three persons: the Father, the Son and the Holy Spirit.

Easter

Easter is the common name for the Christian holiday that celebrates Jesus Christ coming back to life after he died. Like Christmas, Easter in America has both Christian and non-Christian customs. We will first look at the historical events before Jesus' <u>resurrection</u> and then see how other customs were added.

Jesus of Nazareth lived about 33 years (4 BC - 30 AD) in Israel. The Bible says that he was called *the Christ,* meaning "the chosen one" in the Greek language. This name means the same thing as the Hebrew word, "<u>Messiah</u>." The Old Testament, the first part of the Bible, made hundreds of <u>predictions</u> about this Messiah. He would be unlike anyone else ever born on earth. He would be the leader of all God's people. And he would offer eternal life to people.

For a long time Jewish people knew they needed God to <u>forgive</u> them. According to the Bible, all people have disobeyed God. They do not do all the things he says they should do. God's <u>penalty</u> for disobedience is death. The Bible says people cannot earn eternal life because they can never be good enough; they would need to be perfect. However, the death penalty still must be paid. If people pay the penalty themselves, the Bible says they will never be with God. However, God had his own plan – he sent Jesus. Since Jesus obeyed <u>God's Law</u> perfectly, he did not have to die. He did not have to pay the death <u>penalty</u> for himself, so he chose to die for others. Because he was God in human form, unlike anyone else, he was the only one who could do this.

Easter

1st Sunday after full moon after March 21

According to tradition, Jesus was crucified on a Friday. Soldiers nailed his hands and feet to a cross of wood. This was the common form of death for <u>criminals</u> in the Roman Empire. The pain was terrible, and death sometimes did not come for days. Yet Jesus died in only six hours, because soldiers had beaten him earlier. Christians call the day that Jesus died, "Good Friday." This custom began in the fourth century when Christians understood Christ's crucifixion and resurrection as two events, not one. It was "good" to Christians because God kept his promise when Jesus paid the penalty for others. Now it was possible for them to be with God after they died. He paid for their sins.

Friends of Jesus buried him in a small cave used as a grave. The Bible says that early Sunday morning Jesus came back to life. He showed himself to his friends. His body looked the same, and it still had the holes in his hands and feet. He also ate food in front of them (see Luke 24-41-42). But his body had changed – it was now a "spiritual" body – one that would never die again. By coming back alive, Jesus proved that God is stronger than death.

Jesus told his friends that God will forgive any person anywhere who believes or depends on him since he paid the death penalty for them. According to the Bible, faith in Jesus is the requirement for God's forgiveness. Thus Jesus gives them eternal life because of their faith in him.

This message of forgiveness is good news. That is why Christians want to share the message of Easter with others and invite them to Easter church services. Many Christians called this holiday "Resurrection Day." It is their most important holy day. Forty days after his resurrection, Jesus rose up above the earth and went to Heaven. Readers can find the story in the books of Matthew (chapters 26-28), Mark (14-16), Luke (22-24) and John (18-21) in the Bible.

Easter

1st Sunday after full moon after March 21

The date of Easter is different each year. Church leaders in 325 AD used a lunar calendar that is based on the moon's orbit around the earth. It is the first Sunday after the first full moon on or after March 21st. Thus Easter always occurs between March 22nd and April 25th.

As Christians told the Easter message to people from other cultures, different ideas were added to the resurrection celebration. The name "Easter" came from the old German goddess of spring, Eostre. Their spring festival was called Eostur. One can see how this name became Easter.

Celebrating with eggs has been a custom for centuries. In some parts of the world eggs represent the new life that returns during spring season. Ancient Persians and Egyptians colored their eggs in bright colors and gave them to friends as gifts. Christians in the Middle East first used this custom of coloring eggs as part of the Easter celebration. Easter eggs' coloring and styles will be different from country to country. In the United States eggs are also made of chocolate and candy. Empty plastic eggs are filled with small candies and put in Easter baskets. Small children also enjoy looking for hidden Easter eggs. Adults or older children hide eggs in a yard or rooms in a house. Then children find as many eggs as possible and put them into their baskets. The one who finds the most eggs wins a <u>prize</u>.

The "Easter Bunny" also has a long tradition with the holiday. However, like the "Easter eggs," the bunny is related more to the idea of new life from spring, not the resurrection. In ancient Egypt the rabbit represents new life from birth. According to the Egyptians, the rabbit is a symbol of the moon. Since the lunar calendar decides the date of Easter each year, the rabbit or bunny became an Easter symbol. A more modern story about a rabbit came from Germany. There a woman hid Easter eggs for her children during a <u>famine</u>. When the children found the eggs, a big rabbit hopped away. They thought the rabbit brought the eggs. Today many children in the US are told that the "Easter bunny" brings and hides their Easter eggs.

Churches have many special days that come before Easter. *Lent* is the 40-day time to get ready for Easter. During this time people pray, <u>fast</u> or do other religious activities. The first day of *Lent* is called "Ash Wednesday." The day before that is called "Shrove Tuesday." This day is marked by parties, since religious activities begin the next day. The Sunday before Easter is called "Palm Sunday." On this day Jesus' friends made a <u>path</u> of palm branches when he went to Jerusalem on the Sunday before he died. The Thursday before Easter is called "Maundy Thursday." On that night Jesus ate his last and most famous meal. Many churches have special services on these days.

Easter

1st Sunday after full moon after March 21

On Easter Sunday, many Christians attend a sunrise service, sometimes calling it a "Son-Rise" service. The Bible calls Jesus "the Son of God" (Luke 1:35) who would "rise from the dead" (Acts 17:3). Other celebrations include parades, plays, concerts and <u>cantatas</u>. During this time of year people can watch movies on television about the life of Jesus. Some well-known movie titles are *Jesus, Jesus of Nazareth, The Robe, Ben-Hur* and *The Greatest Story Ever Told*. These films can be rented as videos in video stores.

The resurrection of Jesus is the center of the Christian message. If Jesus is still dead and buried, the Bible says that Christians have no hope and nothing to believe. Even today no one has discovered the body of Jesus. The Bible says and Christians believe that "He is risen!"

Some people who do not believe the Easter message say Jesus did not rise from the dead. They try to explain what they think happened on Easter morning. Their ideas go against what the Bible says, and no one has ever found Christ's body. Jesus' resurrection is proof for Christians that the God of the Bible is true and real. Easter is the yearly celebration of all they hope for and believe.

Public schools, colleges and universities in America used to have an Easter vacation. That has been replaced by a time off from school that is now called "Spring Break." Many students travel to southern parts of the country and enjoy <u>recreation</u> in warmer, sunny places like the beach.

Vocabulary

*cantata *(noun)* – a musical performance that includes singers with musicians playing piano, organ or other instruments.

criminal *(noun)* – a person who commits a serious crime.

*crucifixion *(noun)* – the event of dying on a cross when a person's hands and feet are nailed to the wood of the cross.

famine *(noun)* – a serious lack of food.

fast *(verb)* – to eat and drink little or nothing.

forgive *(verb)* – to not feel angry towards someone who did something wrong.

goddess *(noun)* – a female god.

*God's law *(noun)* – the ways of God as told in the Bible; the 10 Commandments.

*lunar *(adjective)* – relating to the moon.

Messiah *(noun)* – Hebrew word meaning "the expected king or deliverer of the Jews."

orbit *(noun)* – the path in space of a planet, moon or spacecraft.

path *(noun)* – a narrow way for walking made by repeated use.

penalty *(noun)* – the punishment one receives for breaking a law or a rule, such as having to pay money (a fine) or going to prison.

prediction *(noun)* – a statement about what will happen in the future.

prize *(noun)* – an award presented for wining a competition.

recreation *(noun)* – fun things to do, such as sports, hobbies, and amusements.

requirement *(noun)* – a necessity; something needed.

*resurrection *(noun)* – the rising from the dead, or returning back to life from being dead.

*sins *(noun)* – behaviors and actions that are against God's commands.

Happy April Fool's Day!

—— April Fool's Day ——

April Fool's Day is not an official holiday, but a traditional one with lots of fun. People love it because on this day they play tricks and jokes on others. The history of this holiday begins with an event that occurred over 2,000 years ago.

Julius Caesar, founder of the ancient Roman Empire, started using a <u>solar</u> calendar in 46 BC. He chose April 1st to be the beginning of the New Year, probably because of the arrival of Spring [see New Year's Day]. Since that time, Western countries had used this calendar. However, 1600 years later, this <u>Julian</u> calendar had problems. For example, at two times during the year the length of daylight and darkness of a 24-hour day is equal. This is called the *equinox*. One equinox occurs in the Spring; the other occurs in the Fall. By the 1600's, the equinoxes occurred 10 days away from when the calendar said they would occur! Something had to be done to correct the calendar.

April Fool's Day
DON'T BE A FOOL!
April 1st

On February 24, 1582, Pope Gregory XIII said that people in all Roman Catholic countries should replace the Julian calendar with a new "<u>Gregorian</u>" one that was created by <u>astronomers</u>. Part of the correction included changing October 5th to October 15th. Many people around Europe were afraid that they had lost 10 days of their lives! So they started <u>riots</u> in many cities.

France's King Charles IX was the first European king to change to the new calendar. But he added another change. He moved New Year's Day from April 1st to January 1st. Many people did not agree with these changes. New ideas like this made them feel <u>insecure</u>.

After a while most people slowly accepted January 1st as New Year's Day. But others did not. They continued to celebrate New Year's in the Spring. They began celebrating on March 25th and ended on April 1st. They were not going to forget their old tradition. Soon these people looked very foolish, celebrating New Year's 3 months after January 1st! Faithful Catholics called them "April fools." In France they were called "April Fish." People made fun of them and played jokes on them. Since gifts were given on New Year's Day at that time, surprise gifts and joke gifts were given to the "April fools."

England did not accept the Gregorian calendar until 1752, but the fun and tricks had begun there about 50 years earlier! Jokes, tricks and surprises that do not hurt anyone are the custom of this silly holiday. No fooling!

Vocabulary

astronomer *(noun)* – a scientist who studies the planets, stars, sun, etc. of outer space.

***Gregorian** *(noun)* - of or relating to Gregory.

insecure *(adjective)* - not steady, unsafe.

***Julian** *(adjective)* - of or relating to Julius (Caesar).

riot *(noun)* - an act of violent behavior by a large group.

***solar** *(adjective)* - of or relating to the sun.

Memorial Day

Memorial Day is a truly <u>patriotic</u> holiday that occurs on May 30th, but is celebrated on the last Monday in May. It is a day to remember and honor those who died while they served in the American armed forces. It includes everyone in the military. Earlier this holiday was called Decoration Day. This holiday also is the sign of the beginning of summer.

This holiday had a slow beginning after the American Civil War (1861-1865). About 500,000 Americans died in that war [see Presidents' Day], more than in any other US war. According to tradition, some women of the Confederate States of America (CSA, the southern states that left the <u>Union</u>) chose May 30th to <u>decorate</u> the graves of Civil War soldiers. They decorated the graves of both Union and Confederate soldiers. Then in 1868 General John A. Logan declared May 30th to be a special day to honor those Union soldiers who died in the war. Logan was Commander-in-chief of the Grand Army of the Republic, an organization of the Union's Civil War <u>veterans</u> [see Veterans Day]. They chose "Memorial Day" as the name of the holiday. Many northern states held similar celebrations for years.

Memorial Day

last Monday in May

Responsibilities for Memorial Day activities later passed to the <u>American Legion</u>. The Legion began in Paris in 1919 after World War I. It is the largest American veteran organization, with over 3 million members. Its main purpose is helping veterans.

To raise money for veterans, Legion members began selling little, red flowers called "poppies." People bought them to wear on their clothes and to remember those who died in war. The idea came from Europe. After the war, poppies grew over many battlefields in France, showing the return of life and peace.

As a result, people called the week before Memorial Day, "Poppy Week." They also put poppies on the graves of soldiers. The money earned from selling poppies helped veterans who were wounded in the war. Poppies are not as common today since most of the World War veterans have died and people forgot the meaning of the flowers. Today veterans' organizations raise money in other ways.

In 1971 Congress created a law that made Memorial Day a national holiday. It is celebrated on the last Monday of May all across the US, making another three-day weekend. It first honored those who died in the Civil War, Spanish-American War (1898), World Wars I (1917-18) and II (1941-45), the Korean War (1950-53). It now includes those who died in the Vietnam War (1961-74) and the Persian Gulf War (1991).

Memorial Day celebrations include parades and special programs with speeches, the reading of Abraham Lincoln's "Gettysburg Address" (a short but famous speech for those who died at the battle at Gettysburg, PA in the Civil War) [see Presidents' Day], prayers and moments of silence. <u>Coastal</u> cities with a <u>naval base</u> often have services for <u>sailors</u> who died at sea. They are similar to those that honor soldiers. People will put on the water small model ships that have flowers on them. They are a memorial for those who died at sea. Americans also attend picnics and baseball games, go sightseeing or boating, play sports, cook meals outdoors, and almost any other kind of fun activity. Those who died in the military did so to protect the freedoms Americans have. Memorial Day remembers those who died for their nation.

Vocabulary

*American Legion *(noun)* – an organization of people, mostly war veterans who fought in wars since 1918, that supports young people and other community interests.

coastal *(adjective)* – near the coast, beach or shore.

decorate *(verb)* – to beautify, put up decorations.

*naval base *(noun)* – military station for sailors, fighting ships and related equipment.

*patriotic *(adjective)* – having or showing pride in one's own country.

sailor *(noun)* – a person who works on a ship.

*Union *(noun)* – during the Civil War, a name Northerners used for the United States.

veteran *(noun)* – any person leaving the military service with a record of good behavior.

Mother's Day
Father's Day

Mother's Day is a holiday that celebrates mothers and motherhood. It is celebrated on the second Sunday in May. This holiday was first celebrated in some European countries for years before the idea became popular in America.

Mother's Day in the US began before the Civil War in 1858. That year Mrs. Anna M. Jarvis began her "Mother's Day Work Clubs" in West Virginia. These clubs became a movement of women who worked with doctors as they helped with women's medical needs. Others spread the idea of honoring mothers. Julia Ward Howe first made the suggestion in 1872 of a holiday on June 2nd for mothers. She held a Mother's Day meeting in Boston for several years. Frank Herring of South Bend, Indiana began a movement to have a Mother's Day celebrated in 1904.

Mother's Day

second Sunday in May

However, it was Miss Anna Jarvis, the daughter of Mrs. Anna M. Jarvis, who began a <u>campaign</u> in 1907 to make Mother's Day a national holiday. She chose the second Sunday in May as the date. She also began the custom of wearing a <u>carnation</u>. A colored carnation means the person's mother is alive. A white carnation means the mother is dead. In 1908 churches in Philadelphia, PA and other cities began celebrating Mother's Day. Ministers encouraged the celebration with sermons about the importance of mothers. On May 10, 1908, the General Conference of the Methodist Episcopal Church in Minneapolis, MN declared that Anna Jarvis was the founder of Mother's Day, and that it should be celebrated on the second Sunday in May.

Mother's Day received national attention when President Woodrow Wilson agreed with Congress on May 9, 1914 that the government observe Mother's Day. The next year the president declared Mother's Day a national celebration.

Father's Day is a result of Mother's Day. Sonora Dodd listened to a sermon in church about the new Mother's Day holiday in 1909. Her mother died when Sonora was young, so her father, a farmer and Civil War veteran, raised her and her five siblings by himself. She suggested that the third Sunday in June become the day to honor fathers. She chose this date because her father's birthday was June 19th, the third Sunday of that month.

The first organizations to support Father's Day were churches. They were also the first to celebrate Mother's Day. Ministers on that Sunday spoke about the "manly" side of Christianity and how God acts like a Heavenly Father. But people did not easily accept the idea of Father's Day. For years it was celebrated only in the churches and in some cities. Efforts to make it a national holiday failed. The Congress would not pass a Father's Day declaration. They believed it would look selfish, since all members of Congress at that time were men. Both Presidents Wilson and Calvin Coolidge would not approve it.

For its first 25 years Father's Day was almost a joke to many people. Did fathers really want flowers and greeting cards? No! Then the Associated Men's Wear Retailers of New York City created the National Council for the Promotion of Father's Day. This action finally gave Father's Day national attention. They were smart to do so. Americans spend about $20 million each year on Father's Day gifts, which are mostly neckties.

Father's Day

HAVE U
HUGGED
DAD 2-DAY
???

third Sunday in June

Anna Jarvis regretted creating Mother's Day because it quickly became a money-making holiday for many businesses. President Nixon declared Father's Day a national celebration in 1972. But when Sonora Dodd died in 1978, Father's Day still was not as popular as Mother's Day. The difference can be seen in telephone calls. Mother's Day is the busiest day of the year for long distance telephone calls. But on Father's Day more collect calls are made than any other day of the year!

Vocabulary

campaign *(noun)* – an organized effort by people to reach a goal.

*carnation *(noun)* – a beautiful flower with many blossoms and a long stem.

*collect call *(noun)* – a telephone call that is paid by the one who receives the call.

manly *(adjective)* – having characteristics, such as strength and courage, that are traditionally associated with men.

sibling *(noun)* – a person with the same parents as someone else, brother or sister.

──Independence Day──

Independence Day in America is also known as the Fourth of July. It is a very important national holiday, and one respected in other parts of the world. It was on July 4, 1776 that thirteen <u>American Colonies</u> declared their freedom from England, the most powerful country on earth. No one thought the Colonies could defeat England in war, but they did. The new nation also grew in size and power like no other country in the last 200 years. The first statement that told the world about their new ideas was the Declaration of Independence. Many of these same leaders later wrote the United States Constitution [see Presidents' Day] that created their new government. That government has lasted longer than any other in the world. Because of its success, many other countries respect the US and have tried to copy it. Events that caused the war, The Declaration, and Independence Day, follow.

Many people were moving to the colonies in North America. This made these colonies different from England's other colonies. The <u>First Great Awakening</u> occurred in the middle 1700's. This was a <u>revival</u> of Christianity when tens of thousands of Americans became more interested in the Bible. They joined churches and were happy to obey God. In England, however, there was no revival like this. Americans felt more <u>loyal</u> to God than to England. The British did not like this attitude, especially when Americans disagreed with them.

Independence Day

Americans thought that they should have a greater part in making decisions about their lives. Their greatest problem was the amount of taxes the British wanted. In 1765 Parliament passed a law called the "Stamp Act." It required a tax on all <u>official</u> papers including newspapers. This tax made Americans very angry. They said, "No taxation without representation!" After one year the British government canceled the law, but they were not happy about it. Then they made another law that took away all representation for the Colonies. New tax laws made more Americans even madder than before. Many of the new taxes were changed, but not the tax on tea. Tea was the symbol of the English way of life. The British government would not change the tea tax.

For that reason, in 1773 some colonists had an idea. They made themselves look like Native Americans and secretly went on English ships in Boston harbor. They threw large boxes of tea into the water. This was called the "Boston Tea Party". Colonists in other towns later did the same thing in other harbors.

The colonists knew what the British government would do. They made more laws. These laws made life very hard for the colonists. In 1774 the Colonies knew that they must join together if things got worse. Then they had another idea: every colony would choose representatives and send them Philadelphia, PA for a meeting called the Continental Congress [see Presidents' Day]. Every colony except Georgia sent representatives. They met during September and October and chose which human rights they needed to protect. They chose to stop trading with England and not use British goods. They also agreed to meet in one year if the British government had not improved things by then.

The British were not going to change now. In fact, they knew more must be done! They thought the Colonies wanted to start a war. The king told British General Thomas Gage to take all <u>ammunition</u> away from the Colonists in Concord, MA. 700 British soldiers called "Redcoats" went to nearby Lexington on April 19, 1775. On his famous ride, Paul Revere warned a small group of American <u>patriots</u>. He shouted, "The British are coming!" When the British arrived, the patriots were ready with rifles called "muskets." After a short 15-minute battle, Redcoats killed 8 patriots and wounded 10 more. Only one Redcoat was wounded. This was the battle that fired "the shot heard 'round the world," as <u>poet</u> Ralph Waldo Emerson said later.

Independence Day

July 4th

When the British arrived at Concord, patriots had already moved the ammunition. Another battle followed. This time more patriots were ready to fight. They hid behind trees and bushes, but the British stood out in the open fields in straight lines. By the end of the day, 250 redcoats had been killed. America lost fewer than 100 men. Three months later George Washington became the leader of all the American soldiers, called "the Continental Army." Other battles against the British began later that year in the Canadian cities of Montreal and Quebec. In December the British government declared war on the Colonies.

The British declaration of war only made the American desire for independence stronger. Patriot leader Samuel Adams asked a question that many were already thinking: "Is not America already independent? Why not then declare it?" British writer Thomas Paine's booklet, *Common Sense,* also said the American colonies should be free. Another famous patriot, Patrick Henry, gave an important speech in Virginia where he said, "Give me liberty or give me death!" Some colonies voted for independence.

Then a second meeting of the colonies' representatives began on May 10, 1775 in Philadelphia. They discussed the war against England and independence for the colonies. On June 7 Virginia delegate Richard Henry Lee said, "These United Colonies are, and of a right [should] be . . . free and independent States . . . " Three days later Congress decided to write an independence declaration. They chose five men to write it: John Adams, Benjamin Franklin, Thomas Jefferson, Robert Livingstone and Roger Sherman. They asked Jefferson to do the writing because they knew he was the best writer in the group. Then the representatives went home to their colonies to better understand the people's thinking.

After returning to Philadelphia, the representatives agreed with Lee's idea about independence on July 2nd. They debated Jefferson's first writing of the declaration, which took him about two weeks to write. He used ideas from church <u>sermons</u> of the day and common political ideas of that time. John Adams called it, "time's greatest debate of all." They made two, very small but important changes. Then after long discussions and a lot of prayer, they approved it on July 4, 1776. John Hancock was the first to write his name on the Declaration of Independence. Others did the same after him. After they all signed it, some men cried. Some looked out the window. Others <u>stared</u> at the floor. Samuel Adams, representative

Independence Day

July 4th

from Massachusetts, stood up and said, "We have this day <u>restored</u> [God], to Whom alone men [should] be obedient. He [rules from] heaven and . . . from the rising to the setting sun, may His Kingdom come."

After representatives voted to approve the Declaration, John Adams, who later became America's second president, wrote his wife Abigail. He said that the Fourth of July

> . . . will be the most [remembered] . . . in the history of America. I . . . believe that it will be celebrated by [future] generations, as the great anniversary festival. It [should] be [celebrated] . . . with parade[s], with shows, games, sports, guns, bells, [big fires], and <u>illuminations</u>; from one end of the continent to the other, from this time forward forevermore.

And so it has been. Celebrations include parades, picnics, patriotic speeches, church services, concerts, and lots of fireworks. Over the years many people were hurt and killed by fireworks during the Fourth of July. In the early 1900's many states made laws against using fireworks privately. However, many still celebrate the holiday with fireworks and sometimes shoot guns in the air. American churches often celebrate Independence Day with sermons that show the relationship between <u>civil</u> liberty and spiritual freedom.

Who were these men who created the United States? At least 50 of the 56 men who signed the Declaration were faithful, active Christians who believed the Bible and went to church regularly. Their own writings, as well as their <u>behavior</u>, prove this fact. They believed that to obey God they must fight <u>tyranny</u>. They only wanted to put the government back in its proper place under God's control. God is mentioned six times in the Declaration. The opening sentence of the Declaration says, "We hold these truths to be [clearly seen], that all men are created equal, that they are <u>endowed</u> by their Creator with certain [unchangeable] rights . . ." It was the first time words like these were ever used to create a government.

What kind of men were they? Generally they were well educated and wealthy. Twenty-four were lawyers or judges. Eleven were merchants, nine were farmers who owned large plantations. Yet they all signed the Declaration of Independence and promised: "For the support of this declaration, with firm <u>reliance</u> on the protection of the Divine Providence [God], we <u>mutually</u> pledge to each other, our lives, our fortunes, and our sacred honor." They knew the penalty would be death if the British captured them.

Most of them suffered terrible losses for leading the colonies to freedom. Five were captured as traitors, and <u>tortured</u> before they died. Twelve had their homes burned. Nine fought and died of injuries from the war. Four of the founders' wives died and two lost their sons who were killed in the battle. Others died in <u>poverty</u>. The cost of freedom for Americans was very high.

Some have questioned if the United States is (or ever was) a Christian nation. For example, people say that the Constitution, the document that created the government, has no ideas in it from the Bible. However, Declaration signer John Adams wrote, "Our Constitution was designed only for a moral and religious people. It is wholly inadequate for the government of any other." One thing is clear: from the very beginning the United States was formed by men who got their ideas about man and government from the Bible.

Many people today say that the long life of America's government is proof that God's ideas about government work best. For over 200 years religious and nonreligious Americans have enjoyed many freedoms and human rights. The Constitution created many freedoms including worship, speech and private property. America is a country of laws that protect these freedoms. In America everyone should obey the laws. Early Americans believed that mankind was evil and needed these laws for society to be successful. These ideas are found in the Bible.

Independence Day

July 4th

There is a battle being fought these days for the future of America. The question is, "What kind of ideas should be the basis for modern American society?" History clearly shows that Christian ideas helped create the country. Since that is true, it should be clear that Christian ideas will help protect our country and guide the future of America in the 21st Century.

Vocabulary

*American Colonies *(noun)* – the eastern part of North America settled by English people during the 17th and 18th Centuries.

ammunition *(noun)* – things that can be fired from a gun or exploded, such as bullets, cannon shells, etc.

*behavior *(noun)* – the actions of a person.

civil *(adjective)* – (in law) of a citizen's rights and responsibilities.

*endow *(verb)* – to richly provide for.

*First Great Awakening *(noun)* – an event in the 18th Century when many thousands of people in the American Colonies became excited about and interested in Christianity.

illumination *(noun)* – something that gives light.

loyal *(adjective)* – faithful to others, especially to one's friends or country.

*mutually *(adverb)* – doing something with the same feeling towards each other.

official *(adjective)* – of or related to a position of power or authority.

patriot *(noun)* – a person who is proud of his or her country and eager to defend it.

poet *(noun)* – a person who writes poems.

poverty *(noun)* – the lack of money and property, the state of being poor.

*reliance *(noun)* – attitude of dependence or being dependent.

restore *(verb)* – to make something look like it did when it was new.

*revival *(noun)* – an event when people renew their interest in obeying God, joining churches and following biblical teachings.

sermon *(noun)* – a speech by a religious leader.

stare *(verb)* – to look at someone or something steadily.

torture *(verb)* – to abuse physically and cause great pain.

*tyranny *(noun)* – the abuse of governmental power; an illegal, cruel or brutal act by the government.

—— American Birthdays ——

Birthdays in America are very common and happy events. Birthday parties are celebrated on the day of the month a person was born. Most often birthdays are celebrated at home with family members and friends.

For larger birthday parties, invitations are sent to announce when and where the party will be. Every birthday party has a birthday cake with candles on it. The number of candles represents the age of the person who has the birthday. The candles are lit and everyone sings the song, "Happy Birthday." Then the person makes a wish (or sometimes three wishes) and then blows out all the candles with one breath so that the wishes will come true. Sometimes a friend will <u>toast</u> the birthday person.

Usually everyone who comes to a birthday party brings a gift and a birthday card for the birthday person. Sometimes flowers are a nice gift. So are books, clothing, music <u>CDs</u> or videos or perfume. For a child's birthday, toys are good gifts. It is good to ask the parents of the birthday child what kind of gifts are right for the child.

Children will wear birthday hats at a child's birthday party. Usually these children will receive a small <u>souvenir</u> from the birthday child. Sometimes a child's party will be celebrated at school with his friends. Cake, ice cream and candy are traditional for a child's party. Pizza, hamburgers and hot dogs are popular for birthday parties. Some parents will take their child to a special restaurant or <u>reserve</u> a special room in a restaurant to celebrate their child's birthday.

Some birthdays in America are special. When girls turn 16 years old, they will have a "Sweet Sixteen" birthday party. The eighteenth birthday is important because children become legal adults on that day. As adults they can vote, drive a car and conduct personal business for themselves. In the US the legal age to drink alcohol is different from state to state. In most states it is twenty-one, so the twenty-first birthday sometimes is another special celebration.

Some people who plan a birthday for someone don't want the birthday person to find out about it. This is called a "surprise party." A friend or family member takes the birthday person to where the party is, but they are not told the reason. When they arrive at the location, everyone is usually hiding. Then they all shout "SURPRISE!"

Birthday parties are a good way to tell people how special they are. It is a way to honor them. If you cannot attend a friend's birthday party, it is good to call them on the telephone and <u>wish</u> them "Happy Birthday," or mail them a birthday card or present.

Vocabulary

CD *(noun)* – abbreviation for compact disc.

reserve *(verb)* – to save a place in a hotel room, on an airplane, etc.

souvenir *(noun)* – an object bought to remember a place (or event).

toast *(verb)* – to honor someone (or something), especially with a drink.

wish *(verb)* – to express hope for something.

Resources

American Heritage Dictionary (1992: Houghton Mifflin Company).

Democracy in America by Alexis de Tocqueville (1945: Vintage Books/Random House; Toronto, Canada).

Grolier's Academic American Encyclopedia (1994: Grolier Electronic Publishing).

Habits of the Heart by Robert Bellah, Richard Madsen, William Sullivan, Ann Swindler, Steven Tipton (1985: University of California Press; Berkeley, CA).

How Now Shall We Live? by Charles Colson and Nancy Pearcey (1999: Tyndale House Publishers; Wheaton, IL).

Never Before In History by Gary Amos and Richard Gardiner (1998: Haughton Publishing Company; Dallas, TX).

Sounding Forth the Trumpet by Peter Marshall and David Manuel (1997: Baker Book House; Grand Rapids, MI).

The Basic Newbury House Dictionary of American English, Philip M. Rideout, Chief Editor (1998: Monroe Allen Publishers, Inc.; Boston, MA).

The Light and the Glory by Peter Marshall and David Manuel (1977: Fleming H. Revell Co., Tarrytown, NY).

The Illustrated Bible and Church Handbook, Stanley I. Stuber, ed. (1966: Association Press, New York, NJ).

The World Book Encyclopedia (1976: Field Enterprises Educational Corporation, Chicago, IL; 1976).